Courageous Christianity

How a 19th century revival sparked the Muscular Christianity movement, Y.M.C.A. athletics, and a youth-led race to save the world

∽

**William J. Federer
R. Michael Federer**

Copyright 10/21/25 William J. Federer, R. Michael Federer. All rights reserved. Conditions of Use: Permission granted to duplicate less than 5,000 words provided acknowledgment is given:

Courageous Christianity: How a 19th century revival sparked the Muscular Christianity movement, Y.M.C.A. athletics, and a youth-led race to save the world

Library of Congress
WORLD HISTORY / UNITED STATES HISTORY
ISBN: 978-1-7369590-8-4

Amerisearch, Inc.
1-888-USA-WORD, 314-502-8924
richmfederer@gmail.com
www.AmericanMinute.com

Dedicated to Charlie Kirk

"I want to be remembered for courage for my faith. That would be the most important thing. The most important thing is my faith."

∽

President Donald J. Trump awarded Charlie Kirk posthumously the Presidential Medal of Freedom, America's highest civilian honor, October 14, 2025:

∽

Erika Kirk received it on behald of her husband, sharing:

"Looking back, these past 12 years of TurningPoint USA ... there's almost this veil of sacredness ... He was ... building a movement ... that called people back to God, back to truth and a movement that was filled with courage ... His confidence in Christ was absolute."

∽

"What we need now is a muscular Christian to make folks sit up and notice."
– *Chariots of Fire,* Eric Liddell's brother urging him to compete in the 1924 Olympics

❦

"Muscular Christians have hold of the old chivalrous and Christian belief, that a man's body is given him to be trained and brought into subjection, and then used for the protection of the weak" – *Tom Brown at Oxford,* 1859

❦

"I can also heartily testify that the safe Guide Book by which one may be led to Christ is the Bible, the Word of God, which is inspired by the Holy Ghost." – Sir George Williams, (1821-1905), Founder of the Young Men's Christian Association

❦

CONTENTS

Introduction 7
It Takes Strength to be Good 9
Rudyard Kipling's Poem "If" 12
Charles G. Finney & The Benevolent Empire 13
Strength to Help Others 28
Sir George Williams founded the Y.M.C.A. 30
Rugby School & Muscular Christianity 39
St. Paul's Athletic Metaphors 45
Olympic Games Revived 47
Y.M.C.A. sent Athletes to Olympics 50
Chariots of Fire 53
Some History of Athletics 56
Oberlin College & the Abolition Movement 60
Layman's Prayer Revival 66
Y.M.C.A. Week of Prayer 71
Rescue Those in Need 72
Y.M.C.A.'s Henri Dunant founded Red Cross 76
Clara Barton founded American Red Cross 80
Y.M.C.A. during Civil War 82
Dwight L. Moody & the Chicago Y.M.C.A. 84
Y.M.C.A. during the Spanish–American War 97
Red Cross during the Spanish-American War 101
Theodore Roosevelt & Moral Strength 102
Rudyard Kipling's Captain Courageous 123
Horatio Alger & Rags to Riches Novels 128
Billy Sunday, Baseball Player turned Preacher 142
Harvest is Plentiful, Laborers are Few 149
William Booth founded the Salvation Army 152
The Gideons Began in a Y.M.C.A. 157
Booker T. Washington founded Tuskegee 157
Frederick Douglass and Self-Made Men 166
Mary Kinnaird: Young Women's Christian Assoc. 168
Dr. Luther H. Gulick, Jr. & Y.M.C.A. Triangle 171
Luther & Lottie Gulick founded Camp Fire Girls . 182
Y.M.C.A.'s James Naismith invented Basketball .. 184

Y.M.C.A.'s William Morgan invented Volleyball. 202
Y.M.C.A. Chapters around the World 207
Jack Boyd, Y.M.C.A. Director 210
Y.M.C.A. led in Racial Reconciliation 215
First Father's Day 218
Y.M.C.A. during World War I 219
Young Men's Hebrew Association 225
Red Cross during World War I 227
Evangeline Booth and the Salvation Army 228
Rev. Edgar Helms founded Goodwill Industries ... 230
A.T. Pierson: Evangelize the World in this Generation 233
John R. Mott, Y.M.C.A. World Committee 239
Lord Baden Powell founded the Boy Scouts 248
Boy Scouts of America 256
Juliette Low founded the Girl Scouts 275
Toastmasters 277
Dale Carnegie, Win Friends & Influence People ... 278
Y.M.C.A. during Depression and World War II 290
Fellowship of Christian Athletes 293
Strength to Do Your Duty 297
Senate Chaplain Peter Marshall, Need For Heroes 302
Erika Kirk – A Commissioning 305
General MacArthur – A Father's Prayer 306

"Spirit-Mind-Body ... The triangle stands ... for the symmetrical man, each part developed with reference to the whole ... What authority have we for believing that this triangle idea is correct? It is Scriptural." –Dr. Luther Gulick, Jr., (1865-1918) Director, Y.M.C.A. Training School

INTRODUCTION

"Do not be conformed to this world, but be transformed by the renewal of your mind, that by testing you may discern what is the will of God, what is good and acceptable and perfect." Romans 12:2

What if there were a pathway to becoming a better steward, not just of oneself, but of one's family, community, and nation? What if there were a set of steps that, if followed properly, takes one from childhood to maturity, from dull to sharpened, from boy to man.

Throughout history, we notice similarities among inspiring and memorable figures. It's as if they knew just the right steps to take to develop the ethos, logos, and pathos, – the honorable intentions, skills, and passions – that made them impactful amongst their peers.

Dr. Wayne Dyer popularized the archetypal stages of one's life if lived properly. The first archetype is "The Athlete"– ambitious and strong, but impressed by themselves and focused on refining their own skills.

After those skills are refined, "the Athlete" takes them into the battlefield of life as "the Warrior" archetype. This where most people spend their lives; using a set of skills they have developed to go into the world and secure only what they need to survive.

There are some however, that continue past this stage. They recognize God's call on their life, then do such a good job of taking care of what they have been entrusted with, that blessings pile up and begin to overflow.

Out of abundance, they begin to naturally seek to improve the lives of others. They "fill their cup so full that it begins to overflow into the cups of others." This is known as "the Statesman" archetype, where a person has been faithful with what they've been given to the point of abundance and now desire to help others.

Each of the men and woman you will read about in this book have reached the "Statesman and Beyond" archetype, focusing on the well-being of others. But how did they arrive there?

In this book, you will see patterns in lives of these successful, inspiring individuals, embodied by the 1800s movement known as "Muscular Christianity." Each of their stories is unique, but all of them recognize that by taking care of "their temple," they invite a healthier mentality.

By improving one's mentality, they are able to create meaningful connections and capitalize on opportunities that invite more tangible blessings into their lives. These blessings and connections then foster a sense of well-being, a sense that you are on the right path and can weather any storm, and a feeling that could be described as being in "perpetually good spirits."

By refining one's "body, mind, and spirit," while avoiding the pitfalls of vanity, you accept God's call on your life and begin to become the best version of yourself; the sharpened sword for the Lord you were called to be, making all your efforts more impactful.

> For the word of God is living and active, sharper than any two-edged sword, piercing to the division of soul and of spirit, of joints and of marrow, and discerning the thoughts and intentions of the heart. (Hebrews 4:12)

In the grand scheme, taking care of one's body is arguably least important, while impacting others is arguably most important. However, by taking care of one's "temple," you invite a cascade of benefits that refreshes your mind, fortifies your spirit, and orients you to the task of uplifting others.

As your cup is filled, you become more capable of filling the cups of others. Enjoy these inspiring stories and discover the undeniable pathway to *Courageous Christianity*.

> And I heard the voice of the Lord saying, "Whom shall I send, and who will go for us?" Then I said, 'Here I am! Send me." (Isaiah 6:8)

IT TAKES STRENGTH TO BE GOOD

Jordan Peterson, a best-selling clinical psychologist, was interviewed by award-winning commentator John Stossel:

Peterson: "It's very helpful for people to hear that they should make themselves competent and dangerous and take the proper place in the world."

Stossel: "Competent and dangerous! Why dangerous?"

Peterson: "Because it's the alternative to being weak and weak is not good."

Stossel: "By dangerous that implies I should be ready to threaten someone to hurt somebody."

Peterson: "No you should be capable of it, but that doesn't mean you should use it. Those who have swords and know how to use them, but keep them sheathed, will inherit the world.
That's a way better way of thinking about it. There's nothing to you otherwise … If you're not a formidable force there's no morality in your self-control.
If you're incapable of violence, not being violent isn't a virtue. Capacity for danger and the capacity for control is what brings about the virtue.
Otherwise you confuse weakness with moral virtue. I'm harmless therefore I'm good. It's like, no, that isn't how it works. That isn't how it works at all. If you're harmless, you're just weak and if you're weak, you're not going to be good.
You can't be because it takes strength to be good. It's very difficult to be good."

Award-winning actor Keanu Reeves was on The Drew Barrymore Show, December 21, 2021:

> Drew: I'm not a fighter. I'm a lover.
> Keanu: No, no. Because if you are a lover you have got to be a fighter.
> Drew: How so?
> Keanu: Because if you don't fight for your love what kind of love do you have?

Where did the idea come from that being weak in the struggle against evil was somehow virtuous?

Was it from Eastern religions, whose adherents were absorbed in self-focused perfection? Was it from the ancient heresy of Gnosticism, where the physical world was bad and only the spiritual world was good?

Was it from religious pietism, whose followers withdrew from "the sinful world" so much they effectively gave their tacit approval to injustice by their cowardly non-involvement?

How can a weak person carry out the commands:

> Psalm 82:4 "Rescue the weak and the needy; deliver them from the hand of the wicked."

> Proverbs 24:11–12 "Rescue those who are being taken away to death."

> Psalm 82:3 "Defend the defenseless, the fatherless and the forgotten. Protect the rights of the oppressed and the poor."
> Isaiah 1:17 "Rebuke the oppressor; defend the orphan. Plead for the widow."

> Jeremiah 22:3 " Deliver those who have been robbed from those who oppress them."

Isaiah 58:6–8 "Is not this the kind of fasting I have chosen: to loose the chains of injustice and untie the cords of the yoke, to set the oppressed free and break every yoke?"

How can believers fulfill these Bible commands if they are weak?

༄

RUDYARD KIPLING'S POEM "IF"

Rudyard Kipling, author of *Captains Courageous*, wrote the poem "IF" in 1895:

If you can keep your head when all about you
Are losing theirs and blaming it on you;
If you can trust yourself when all men doubt you,
But make allowance for their doubting too;
If you can wait and not be tired by waiting,
Or, being lied about, don't deal in lies,
Or, being hated, don't give way to hating,
And yet don't look too good, nor talk too wise;
If you can dream – and not make dreams your master;
If you can think – and not make thoughts your aim;
If you can meet with triumph and disaster
And treat those two impostors just the same;
If you can bear to hear the truth you've spoken
Twisted by knaves to make a trap for fools,
Or watch the things you gave your life to broken,
And stoop and build 'em up with worn-out tools;
If you can make one heap of all your winnings
And risk it on one turn of pitch-and-toss,
And lose, and start again at your beginnings
And never breath a word about your loss;
If you can force your heart and nerve and sinew
To serve your turn long after they are gone,

And so hold on when there is nothing in you
Except the Will which says to them: "Hold on";
If you can talk with crowds and keep your virtue,
Or walk with kings — nor lose the common touch;
If neither foes nor loving friends can hurt you;
If all men count with you, but none too much;
If you can fill the unforgiving minute
With sixty seconds' worth of distance run —
Yours is the Earth and everything that's in it,
And, which is more — you'll be a Man, my son!

༄

CHARLES G. FINNEY & THE BENEVOLENT EMPIRE

Just as Charlie Kirk's courage to engage millions of young people using convincing logic sparked a movement championing faith and liberty, two centuries prior, 29-year-old attorney Charles Finney ignited a worldwide revival and a movement to reform society. In the 19th century Second Great Awakening, Finney presented Gospel evidence as a lawyer before a jury, then asked for a verdict. He challenged young people to act out their faith by helping the less fortunate.

Finney's family did not attend church while he was growing up. The few times he did, he found it dispassionate, just mundane intellectualism.

In 1821, Charles Finney was practicing law in Adams, New York. He studied Sir William Blackstone's *Commentaries on the Laws of England*, where he saw so many references to the

Bible that he decided to seek God. He described in his *Memoirs*, how on October 10, 1821:

> Tuesday night I had become very nervous ... a strange feeling came over me as if I was about to die. I knew that if I did I should sink down to hell; but I quieted myself as best I could until morning.
>
> At an early hour I started for the office. But just before I arrived ... something seemed to confront me with questions ... Indeed, it seemed as if the inquiry was within myself, as if an inward voice said to me, "What are you waiting for? Did you not promise to give your heart to God?"
>
> ... I think I then saw, as clearly as I ever have in my life, the reality and fullness of the atonement of Christ. I saw that His work was a finished work; and that instead of having, or needing, any righteousness of my own to recommend me to God, I had to submit myself to the righteousness of God through Christ ...
>
> Salvation, it seemed to me, instead of being a thing to be wrought out by my own works, was a thing to be found entirely in the Lord Jesus Christ ...
>
> Without being distinctly aware of it, I had stopped in the street right where the inward voice seemed to arrest me. How long I remained in that position I cannot say ...
>
> Before my mind, the question seemed to be put, "Will you accept it now, today?" I replied, "Yes; I will accept it today, or I will die in the attempt."

Finney continued:

North of the village, and over a hill, lay a piece of woods, in which I was in the almost daily habit of walking ... As I went over the hill, it occurred to me that some one might see me ... so great was my pride ...

As I turned to go up into the woods, I recollect to have said, "I will give my heart to God, or I never will come down from there" ... Just at that point this passage of Scripture seemed to drop into my mind with a flood of light:

"Then shall ye go and pray unto me, and I will hearken unto you. Then shall ye seek me and find me, when ye shall search for me with all your heart."

I instantly seized hold of this with my heart. I had intellectually believed the Bible before; but never had the truth been in my mind that faith was a voluntary trust instead of an intellectual state. I was as conscious as I was of my existence, of trusting at that moment in God's veracity.

Somehow I knew that that was a passage of Scripture, though I do not think I had ever read it. I knew that it was God's word, and God's voice, as it were, that spoke to me. I cried to Him,

"Lord, I take thee at thy word. Now thou knowest that I do search for Thee with all my heart, and that I have come here to pray to Thee; and Thou hast promised to hear me" ...

I told the Lord that I should take Him at His word; that He could not lie; and that therefore I was sure that He heard my prayer, and that He would be found of me.

After several hours of prayer, Charles Finney went back to his law office.

> Just at dark Squire Wright (his law partner), seeing that everything was adjusted, bade me good-night and went to his home.
>
> I had accompanied him to the door; and as I closed the door and turned around, my heart seemed to be liquid within me. All my feelings seemed to rise and flow out; and the utterance of my heart was, "I want to pour my whole soul out to God."
>
> The rising of my soul was so great that I rushed into the room back of the front office, to pray. There was no fire, and no light, in the room; nevertheless it appeared to me as if it were perfectly light.
>
> As I went in and shut the door after me, it seemed as if I met the Lord Jesus Christ face to face. It did not occur to me then, nor did it for some time afterward, that it was wholly a mental state.
>
> On the contrary it seemed to me that I saw Him as I would see any other man. He said nothing, but looked at me in such a manner as to break me right down at His feet. I have always since regarded this as a most remarkable state of mind; for it seemed to me a reality, that He stood before me, and I fell down at His feet and poured out my soul to Him.
>
> I wept aloud like a child, and made such confession as I could with my choked utterance. It seemed to me that I bathed His feet with my tears; and yet I

had no distinct impression that I touched Him, that I recollect.

I must have continued in this state for a good while; but my mind was too much absorbed with the interview to recollect anything that I said.

But I know, as soon as my mind became calm enough to break off from the interview, I returned to the front office, and found that the fire that I had made of large wood was nearly burned out.

But as I turned and was about to take a seat by the fire, I received a mighty baptism of the Holy Ghost.

Without any expectation of it, without ever having the thought in my mind that there was any such thing for me, without any recollection that I had ever heard the thing mentioned by any person in the world, the Holy Ghost descended on me in a manner that seemed to go through me, body and soul. I could feel the impression, like a wave of electricity, going through and through me.

Indeed it seemed to come in waves and waves of liquid love; for I could not express it in any other way. It seemed like the very breath of God. I can recollect distinctly that it seemed to fan me, like immense wings.

No words can express the wonderful love that was shed abroad in my heart. I wept aloud with joy and love; and I do not know but I should say, I literally bellowed out the unutterable gushings of my heart.

The waves came over me, and over

> me, one after the other, until I recollect I cried out, "I shall die if these waves continue to pass over me." I said, "Lord, I cannot bear any more;" yet I had no fear of death.

He was startled when someone entered his law office and realized it was morning. He had prayed all night long. A church deacon suing a fellow-church member asked how his case was coming along. Without hesitating, Finney replied:

> I have a retainer from the Lord Jesus Christ to plead his cause, and cannot plead yours.

The deacon was so stung by Finney's rebuke that shortly after he settled his case.

Finney immediately began preaching. He presented the Gospel as a lawyer giving his closing argument. He wrote in his *Autobiography*:

> Great sermons lead the people to praise the preacher. Good preaching leads the people to praise the Savior.

Wherever Finney preached, crime plummeted. Shops closed as people rushed to hear him. New England preacher Lyman Beecher estimated that 100,000 came to the Lord in one year:

> That was the greatest work of God, and the greatest revival of religion, that the world has ever seen, in so short a time.

Lyman Beecher's daughter was Harriet Beecher Stowe, who wrote the anti-slavery novel *Uncle Tom's Cabin*, and his son was the famous anti-slavery preacher, Henry Ward Beecher.

Billy Graham wrote of Finney in the Foreword

of *The Life and Ministry of Charles G. Finney* by Dr. Lewis A. Drummond (Bethany House, 1983):

> Few men have had such a profound impact on their generation as Charles Grandison Finney. Through his Spirit-filled evangelistic ministry, uncounted thousands came to know Christ in the nineteenth century, resulting in one of the greatest periods of revival in the history of America.
>
> In addition, he became one of the most widely-read theologians of his time through his lectures and writings. His concern for education influenced whole generations of students.
>
> But most of all, Charles G. Finney was a deeply-committed Christian. More than anything else he wanted to serve Christ and be used of Him.

In his lifetime, Finney led estimated 500,000 to the Lord. Charles Spurgeon described Finney's preaching in his *Lectures to My Students*, 1875:

> Mr. Finney ... his power lay in his use of clear arguments. Many who knew his fame were greatly disappointed at first hearing him, because he used few beauties of speech and was as calm and dry as a book of Euclid; but he was exactly adapted to a certain order of minds, and they were convinced and convicted by his forcible reasoning.

Finney began the tradition praying in colloquial English rather than in the formal King's English with "thee's" and "thou's." Finney began what came to be known as an "altar call" in his 1830 revival in Rochester, New York, stating:

> I had found, that with the higher classes especially, the greatest obstacle to be overcome was their fear of being known as anxious inquirers. They were too proud ...
>
> Something was needed, to make the impression on them that they were expected at once to give up their hearts; something that would call them to act, and act as publicly before the world, as they had in their sins; something that would commit them publicly to the service of Christ ...
>
> I had called them simply to stand up in the public congregations ... to bring them out from among the mass of the ungodly, to a public renunciation of their sinful ways, and a public committal of themselves to God.

He added:

> The will is, in a sense, enslaved by the carnal and worldly desires. Hence it is necessary to awaken men to a sense of guilt and danger, and thus produce an excitement of counter feeling and desire which will break the power of carnal and worldly desire and leave the will free to obey God.

In his *Systematic Theology*, 1846, Finney explained that the Law shows us we are all sinners and points us to our need for the Lamb of God, who took the judgment for our sins in our place:

> "The Law must prepare the way for the Gospel. To overlook this in instructing souls is almost certain to result in false hope, the introduction of a false standard of

Christian experience, and to fill the church with false converts."

"A law without sanctions is no law; it is only counsel, or advice."

"God works or draws, and the sinner yields or turns, or which is the same thing, changes his heart, or, in other words, is born again. The sinner is dead in trespasses and sins. God calls on him, 'Awake thou that sleepest, arise from the dead that Christ may give thee light.' God calls; the sinner hears and answers, 'Here am I.'"

Finney credited the prayers of an elderly minister, Daniel Nash, and his "praying band," for the success of the revival meetings:

> Father Nash was a most wonderful man in prayer, one of the most earnest, devout, spiritually-minded, heavenly-minded men I ever saw ...
>
> He labored about in many places in central and northern New York, and gave himself up to almost constant prayer, literally praying himself to death at last. I have been informed that he was found dead in his room in the attitude of prayer.

Finney wrote:

> "A revival may be expected when Christians have a spirit of prayer for a revival. That is, when they pray as if their hearts were set upon it. When Christians have the spirit of prayer for a revival ... When they have real travail of soul."

"I laid great stress upon prayer as an indispensable condition of promoting the revival."

"Revival comes from heaven when heroic souls enter the conflict determined to win or die—or if need be, to win and die!"

"When sinners are careless and stupid, and sinking into hell unconcerned, it is time the church should bestir themselves. It is as much the duty of the church to awake, as it is for the firemen to awake when a fire breaks out in the night in a great city."

"When the fallow ground is thoroughly broken up in the hearts of Christians, when they have confessed and made restitution ... if the work be thorough and honest – they will naturally and inevitably fulfill the conditions, and will prevail in prayer ...

What we commonly hear in prayer and conference meetings is not prevailing prayer. It is often astonishing and lamentable to witness the delusions that prevail upon the subject.

Who that has witnessed real revivals of religion has not been struck with the change that comes over the whole spirit and manner of the prayers of really revived Christians?"

"It was very common to find Christians, whenever they met in any place, instead of engaging in conversation, to fall on their knees in prayer."

"Nothing tends more to cement the

hearts of Christians than praying together. Never do they love one another so well as when they witness the outpouring of each other's hearts in prayer."

"There must be a waking up of energy, on the part of Christians, and an outpouring of God's Spirit, or the world will laugh at the church."

"A revival is nothing else than a new beginning of obedience to God."

"You have seen them falling into sin, and you let them go on. And yet you pretend to love them. What a hypocrite! Would you see your wife or child going into disgrace, or into the fire, and hold your peace? No, you would not."

"Whenever sinners are not being saved and believers sanctified, there is a lack of Holy Spirit power.

When will our theological professors and our ministers learn the all-important lesson so illustrated in the Acts of the Apostles and so verified by all the ages, that the chief factor in ministerial success is ... the baptism with the Holy Ghost, the being "filled with the Spirit?"

Finney believed being a Christian meant more than hearing sermons. One should actually be doing something to show their faith, to carry out God's will. An apple tree should sooner or later bring forth apples, as William Tyndale wrote in *Prologues to the New Testament*, 1525-35:

And where God's spirit is not, there can

be no good works, even as where an apple tree is not, there can grow no apples ...

As a good tree bringeth forth good fruit, and an evil tree evil fruit. By the fruits shall ye know what the tree is: a man's deeds declare what he is within ... as the fire must be first hot yer it warm any thing.

Finney formed the Benevolent Empire, a network of volunteer organizations to aid the sick, poor, homeless, and aged. In 1834, it had a budget rivaling the Federal Government.

Affiliated organizations included: American Home Missionary Society; American Temperance Society; American Board of Commissioners for Foreign Missions; American Sunday School Union; American Tract Society; and American Bible Society, which even translated Bibles into Indian languages.

At this time, there were no government welfare programs. It was generous individuals, churches and ministries that cared for the needy.

Finney motivated Christians to show the love of Christ to the world through actions, reforming education, prison systems, insane asylums, bankruptcy laws, and labor laws. This led to the building schools, hospitals, orphanages, free medical dispensaries, homes for the aged, and day camps for children in the slums.

They provided job placement, fought alcohol abuse with the temperance movement, advanced women's rights, formed missionary societies to minister to American Indians and overseas, and founded abolitionist societies to end slavery.

Some, though, focused so much on doing good, a Gospel of works, that they neglected preaching the Gospel of grace, giving rise to the secular social reform movement.

Finney wrote in the *Oberlin Evangelist*:

> The Christian church was designed to ... lift up her voice and put forth her energies against iniquity in high and low places - to reform individuals, communities, and governments.

On October 5, 1824, Charles married Lydia Andrews. Three days later he preached a revival. Charles and Lydia had five children. Though reserved, Lydia organized women's prayer meetings, which to Charles were key to a revival's success. Each town where there were revivals, Lydia formed maternal associations and schools.

In 1831, Finney preached in New York's Second Free Presbyterian Church, then organized Chatham Street Chapel, which became Broadway Tabernacle. His preaching fueled the abolitionist movement, with the church's motto being: "Slavery and Christianity cannot live together."

Finney's influence continued with the church's following pastor, Rev. Dr. Joseph P. Thompson, preaching "It is necessary to wipe out Slavery, from the South ... It is prying upon our vitals, and must be cut out with the sharp edge of the sword." He raised funds for a "church regiment" to join the Union Army in the fight to end slavery.

Finney wrote in his *Memoirs,* published 1876:

> I had made up my mind on the question of slavery, and was exceedingly anxious

to arouse public attention to the subject ...
> In my prayers and preaching, I so often alluded to slavery, and denounced it, that a considerable excitement came to exist among the people.

Finney inspired John Jay Shipherd to found Oberlin College in 1833, a center of abolitionism.

Finney inspired Titus Coan to be a missionary to Hawaii in 1834, resulting in thousands of conversions in the Hawaiian Great Awakening.

Finney began teaching at Oberlin in 1837 and became its president in 1851. Lydia, set a new model for minister's wives by being active in Oberlin's women's department. She was viewed by students as a "mother confessor" and spiritual advisor. She set up a women's network for missions and anti-slavery activism.

Oberlin's campus became part of the Underground Railroad, smuggling slaves to freedom. Finney wrote that schools:

> Should be allowed to receive colored people on the same conditions that they did white people; that there should be no discrimination on account of color.

When Lydia died, December 17, 1847, Charles called it his darkest hour.

A widow, Elizabeth Atkinson, met Finney and they married November 13, 1848. She recruited women to be active in prayer meetings, which Charles described as "one of the most important instrumentalities in the promotion of a revival." Her tireless participation led Finney to popularize the idea of a team ministry. At her insistence,

Charles went to England, where he influenced George Williams to found the Y.M.C.A.

Finney wrote of the Kingdom of God:

> "Every member must work or quit. No honorary members."

> "It is the great business of every Christian to save souls."

> "He that winneth souls is wise (Proverbs 11:30) - Those are the best educated ministers, who win the most souls."

> "By precept and example, on every proper occasion, by their lips, but mainly by their lives ... Christians have no right to be silent with their lips; they should rebuke, exhort, and entreat with all long-suffering and doctrine. But their main influence as witnesses is by their example."

Finney wrote in Lecture XV "Hindrances to Revival" (*Lectures on Revival*, 1855):

> Politics are a part of religion in such a country as this, and Christians must do their duty to the country as a part of their duty to God. It seems sometimes as if the foundations of the nation were becoming rotten, and Christians seem to act as if they thought God did not see what they do in politics.
>
> But I tell you, He does see it, and He will bless or curse this nation, according to the course they take."

STRENGTH TO HELP OTHERS

Finney's *Lectures on Revivals of Religion,* 1835, inspired William and Catherine Booth to found The Salvation Army in 1865, and George Williams to found the Y.M.C.A.–Young Men's Christian Association in 1844. Benevolent Empire inspired the founding of The Salvation Army, the Y.M.C.A., the Red Cross, and similar volunteer organizations created for the purpose of helping those in need.

The attitude was that Word God gives commands to five groups: individuals, families, businesses, the church, and government.

Individuals, among other things, are instructed to be generous and charitable, helping poor strangers as "good Samaritans."

Family commands have a different focus, being mostly relational, such as husbands love your wives, children obey your parents, and provide for those of your own household.

Business commands stress being fair, do an honest days work, and do not hold back wages.

Church commands include caring for the poor, and immediately, it did. The Book of Acts describes the church feeding widows. The Book of James defines pure religion as caring for the fatherless and widows. Over the centuries, churches helped the homeless, infirmed, maimed, outcasts, delinquents, strangers, immigrants, visiting the sick, imprisoned, shut-ins, and later founded hospitals and schools.

Surprisingly, there are no commands for the government to take care of the poor, or get involved in education, or healthcare, or provide jobs. The government's role is the simplest: protect the innocent and punish the guilty.

What has happened is the government usurped the church's role. When the church gets weaker it allows the government to get stronger. If church members are strong and successful, does not that put them in a better position to help those in need?

When churches help people it is called "disinterested benevolence." When governments help, by taking from some and dispensing to others, there is a problem. Governments are run by political bureaucrats who want to keep their powerful jobs. They are tempted to dispense benefits in a discretionary way, in exchange for votes.

James Madison told Congress, 1794:

> Charity is no part of the legislative duty of the government.

Coolidge warned, May 15, 1926:

> The Federal Government ought to resist the tendency to be loaded up with duties which the states should perform. It does not follow that because something ought to be done, the national government ought to do it.

Congressman Davy Crockett gave a speech "Not Yours to Give," April 2, 1828:

> Congress has not the power to appropriate this money as an act of charity ...
>
> We have the right as individuals, to give away as much of our own money as we please in charity; but as members of Congress we have no right to appropriate

a dollar of the public money ... as charity.

President Grover Cleveland vetoed a Texas Seed Bill in 1887:

> I do not believe that the power ... of the general government ought to be extended to the relief ...
>
> Charity of our countrymen can always be relied upon to relieve their fellow-citizens in misfortune ... Federal aid, in such cases, encourages the expectation of paternal care on the part of the government and weakens the sturdiness of our national character.

President Gerald Ford stated March 11, 1976:

> People say ... why don't you expand that program, why don't you spend more Federal money? ... I don't think they have understood one of the fundamentals ...
>
> I look them in the eye and I say,
>
> "Do you realize that a government big enough to give us everything we want is a government big enough to take from us everything we have?"

SIR GEORGE WILLIAMS FOUNDED THE Y.M.C.A.

In the 19th century, meeting social needs was championed by spiritually-motivated church members. Volunteer organizations were formed, one of the most well-known being the Y.M.C.A.

Many are familiar with the song released by the Village People in 1978, which experienced a resurgence by being performed at political rallies and at the pre-inauguration event with President Donald J. Trump on stage, January 19, 2025.

Few, though, are aware of the spiritual origins of the Y.M.C.A.

George Williams was born October 11, 1821, on a farm in Dulverton, Somerset, England. Though baptized in the Church of England, he described himself as "a careless, thoughtless, godless, swearing young fellow." His parents sent him to the town of Bridgwater to be an apprentice at a draper's shop, a type of department store.

In 1837, Williams converted from Anglicanism to Congregationalism and became an active member of the Zion Congregational Church.

In 1841, at the age of 20, he moved to London to work at Hitchcock & Rogers draper shop. He attended King's Weigh House Congregational Church, and became active evangelizing.

Working as a cloth merchant, he was promoted to department manager. Then he read Charles Finney's *Lectures on Revival* and was motivated him to give his life in service of the Lord.

His nephew, Sir John Ernest Hodder-Williams, wrote in *The Father of the Red Triangle, The Life of Sir George Williams, Founder of the Y.M.C.A.*, 1918:

> And then ... enters the famous and startling figure of the Rev. Charles G. Finney, the American evangelist ...
> When Finney was conducting his second campaign in London, George

Williams attended his meetings, but it was through Finney's books — his *Lectures to Professing Christians* and his *Lectures on Revivals of Religion* — that this man's remarkable personality first entered the spiritual homeland of George Williams.

What power for good still lies and shall ever lie in a good book! ... To these printed lectures by Finney are certainly due much of the zeal and passion which produced the Young Men's Christian Association.

These books were first published in 1837, and must have fallen into George Williams's hands in the first glow of his religious faith. They fanned it into a flame which became a devouring fire. For such a young man, no more inspiring works could have been found.

George Williams was not a student, not a great reader; matters of criticism and details of doctrine always failed to excite his interest. He knew nothing and cared nothing about the results of linguistic or historical inquiry into the authenticity of the Scriptures ...

Once the decision made, no questionings seemed to trouble him. He was disturbed by no doubts ... There was nothing of complacency in his nature; his conscience was very tender. What he believed, he believed with all his might ...

In Finney's books you will find the secret, not only of George Williams' assurance of faith, but also of his absorbing passion for souls and for the work that wins souls ...

To Finney the great business on earth of

every Christian was to save souls. "If you are thus neglecting the main business of life," he writes," what are you living for?"

I have quoted these few phrases from Finney's books because they are little known by the younger generations, and because ... they did much to mold and make George Williams what he was ...

He absorbed Finney's creed. To him, from the day of his conversion, to live was Christ and to bring to Christ all with whom he came in contact; in season, out of season, always, everywhere, to preach Christ.

England's Industrial Revolution, 1760 to 1840, saw railroads bring rural young men into crowded cities for work. They labored ten to twelve hours a day, six days a week. Far from home, many lived at their workplace, stacked in rooms above company shops or in tenements. Streets were filled with unhealthy social conditions, open sewers, drunks, thugs, beggars, pickpockets, gangs of abandoned children running wild, sinful taverns, with temptations of illicit love.

Williams wrote of the appalling immoral conditions tempting young working men:

> They were treated as though deprived of mind ... as though formed only to labor and sleep ... without a moment for spiritual or mental culture, without the disposition or even the strength for the performance of those devotional exercises which are necessary to the maintenance of a spiritual life.

On June 6, 1844, 22-year-old George Williams brought together a dozen young men to meet above a drapery shop in St. Paul's Churchyard in London, England, to found the first Y.M.C.A.

It was a place where young men could go and not be tempted into sin, but instead be a "refuge of Bible study and prayer for young men seeking escape from the hazards of life on the streets."

This was an interdenominational organization integrating athletics with prayer and Bible study. William named it the Young Men's Christian Association. He sought to include Christians from different churches and social classes.

Within seven years, the Y.M.C.A. had 24 chapters across Britain with 2,700 members of all denominations, races, and social classes.

It was the beginning of the 19th century movement known as "Muscular Christianity," which led to the concept of "good sportsmanship."

In 1851, the Young Men's Christian Association set up a booth at the Crystal Palace Exposition, which drew visitors from all over the world.

An American seaman and missionary, Captain Thomas Valentine Sullivan, brought the Y.M.C.A. to the United States, opening the country's first chapter in Boston's Old South Church in 1851, so that young Christian sailors on shore leave could have a safe and moral "home away from home."

Within two years it had 1,500 members. Its first president, Franklin W. Smith, was a hardware merchant and abolitionist. It started an Evening Institute for Younger Men to provide an education for "any young man of moral character," which evolved into Northeastern University of Boston.

Within a year, Y.M.C.A. chapters were founded in Montreal, Canada; Baltimore, Maryland; Paris,

France; and Geneva, Switzerland.

In 1853, there were thirteen Y.M.C.A.s in America. In Washington, D.C., Anthony Bowen, a slave who had purchased his freedom, opened a chapter to serve the African American community. It was the first black institution in America other than churches.

In London, one of George William's earliest converts was his employer, George Hitchcock, who generously supported the movement.

In 1853, Williams married Hitchcock's daughter, Helen Jane Maunder Hitchcock, and together they had seven children.

Hitchcock made Williams a partner in the business, renaming it George Hitchcock, Williams & Co. After Hitchcock's death in 1863, Williams inherited the business.

By 1855, just eleven years after the first meeting, there were 329 Y.M.C.A. chapters in nine countries with 30,360 members.

That year, 100 delegates met at the first Y.M.C.A. World Conference, hosted in the Paris. They formed the International Y.M.C.A., adopting the Paris Basis, with the goal:

> ...to unite those young men who, regarding Jesus Christ as their God and Savior according to the Holy Scriptures, desire to be His disciples in their doctrine and in their life, and to associate their efforts for the extension of His Kingdom amongst young men.

In 1856, the first student-led Y.M.C.A. were at Cumberland University in Lebanon, Tennessee, then at Milton Academy, in Milton, Wisconsin.

The Cincinnati Y.M.C.A. began the nation's first English as a Second Language Class for German immigrants.

In 1861, at the start of the Civil War, President Lincoln asked for Y.M.C.A. volunteers. Over 5,000 responded from 15 northern Y.M.C.A. chapters, forming the U.S. Christian Commission. They cared for troops and prisoners of war, serving as medics, nurses, and chaplains, distributing food, clothing, and medical supplies.

In 1866, New York City's Y.M.C.A. adopted as its mission "the improvement of the spiritual, mental, social, and physical condition of young men." In 1869, it added a bowling alley and gym in its building, considered the nation's first indoor sports facility.

In 1867, Chicago's Y.M.C.A. opened Farwell Hall, the first Y.M.C.A. with a dormitory, with 42 rooms. This became a model for other chapters, and by 1940, there were 100,000 Y.M.C.A.s dorm rooms nationwide – more than any hotel chain.

In 1869, America had 659 Y.M.C.A. chapters. In Massachusetts, the Salem Y.M.C.A. began the first Boys' Work Department, programs for male youths 12 to 18 years old.

In 1869, Howard University had the first black student Y.M.C.A.

In 1875, the San Francisco Y.M.C.A. was opened to serve the Asian communities. Y.M.C.A. secretaries were immigrants from China who had converted to Christianity. They felt the intolerance of the Chinese Exclusion Act of 1882. In 1917, a Japanese Y.M.C.A. opened in San Francisco.

In 1878, the first Y.M.C.A. was founded in

Jerusalem. That year, the international Y.M.C.A. headquarters opened in Geneva, Switzerland. The Y.M.C.A. emblem named the five parts of the world: Europe, Asia, Oceania, Africa and America.

In 1879, the first Y.M.C.A. to serve native American communities was opened in Flandreau, South Dakota by Thomas Wakeman, son of Chief Little Crow. By 1885, there were 10 native American Y.M.C.A.s in the Dakota, Minnesota, Nebraska, and Carlisle, PA. In 1895, the Y.M.C.A. hired the first native American, Dr. Charles Eastman, a Sioux who graduated from Dartmouth and Boston University's School of Medicine. By 1898, there were 40 Indian Y.M.C.A. chapters.

In 1879, a Y.M.C.A. began at Fort Snelling in St. Paul, giving soldiers moral, friendly support away from temptations.

In 1881, the Y.M.C.A. in San Francisco founded a Night School, renamed in 1895 to Y.M.C.A. Evening College. In 1910, it added Y.M.C.A. Law School, and in 1923, it was renamed Golden Gate College.

In 1885, the Y.M.C.A. School for Christian Workers was opened in Springfield, Massachusetts. It was renamed the International Y.M.C.A. Training School. That year, the Brooklyn Central Y.M.C.A. had the first pool, and by the end of the year, 17 chapters had pools.

In 1885, one of America's first permanent summer camps for boys was the Y.M.C.A.'s Camp Dudley, in Orange Lake, New York.

The Y.M.C.A was a volunteer organization of adult Christian men, but exploding membership created the need secretaries. In 1886, Ellen Brown was hired as the first female Y.M.C.A. employee, to be secretary for the Boy's Work department.

In 1886, D.L. Moody's Mount Hermon Boys' School near Northfield, Massachusetts, hosted 250 Y.M.C.A. students. After a stirring sermon, 100 students, known thereafter as the Mount Hermon Hundred, volunteered to be missionaries to "evangelize the world in a generation." They signed the pledge: "We hold ourselves willing and desirous to do the Lord's work wherever He may call us, even if it be in the foreign lands."

This began the Student Volunteer Movement for Foreign Missions, one of the most significant events in missions history, with over 20,000 of youth going to the mission field in the next two decades.

In 1888, the Y.M.C.A. hired the first full-time black secretary, William Hunton. In 1896, there were 60 black Y.M.C.A.s. The first conference of black Y.M.C.A. secretaries was in 1900. By 1924, there were 160 black Y.M.C.A.s, built with the help of the Jewish part-owner of the Sear, Roebuck and Company, Julius Rosenwald.

In 1890, Y.M.C.A. Institute and Training Schools began in Chicago and Lake Geneva, Wisconsin.

The Y.M.C.A. has grown to be the oldest and largest youth charity in the world, with 10,000 chapters in 124 countries with 64 million members.

In 1894, George Williams, after 50 years of bringing young men to Christ, was knighted by Queen Victoria. He died November 6, 1905, and was buried in London's historic St. Paul's Cathedral. A stained-glass window honors him in Westminster Abbey.

In Montreal, Canada, the Y.M.C.A. founded

Sir George Williams University. It later merged into Concordia University, though it retained the campus name "Sir George Williams Campus."

Concerned with keeping young men from temptation, Sir George Williams stated:

> My life-long experience as a business man, and as a Christian worker among young men, has taught me that the only power in this world that can effectually keep one from sin, in all the varied and often attractive forms ... is that which comes from an intimate knowledge of the Lord Jesus Christ as a present Savior ...
>
> And I can also heartily testify that the safe Guide–Book by which one may be led to Christ is the Bible, the Word of God, which is inspired by the Holy Ghost.

Psalm 119:9 states:

> How can a young man cleanse his way?
> By taking heed according to Your word.

RUGBY SCHOOL & MUSCULAR CHRISTIANITY

George Williams' vision of being spiritual and physical fit fueled the movement for young men to have strength, stamina, and good character so as to better equip them to better serve others.

It espoused qualities such as discipline, self-sacrifice, chivalry, moral principles and patriotic duty. These virtues grew in esteem during England's Victorian Era, 1837–1901.

The term "muscular Christianity" was coined in 1857 by the English barrister Thomas Collett Sandars in his review of the novel *Two Years Ago.*

In the novel, written by Anglican clergyman Charles Kingsley, the characters displayed gallantry, self-reliance, resilience, and denounced slavery. Kingsley wrote of sports:

> Games conduce, not merely to physical, but to moral health.

Another author whose novels espoused muscular Christianity was Ralph Connor, a missionary in the harsh frontiers of Western Canada. He praised his family's Scottish immigrant values of dauntless determination, tireless hard work, a stern Calvinism faith and a wry wit.

In 1895, the *London Quarterly and Holborn Review* described the adventurous British explorer John MacGregor, also known as Rob Roy:

> John MacGregor is perhaps the finest specimen of Muscular Christianity that this or any other age has produced. Three men seemed to have struggled within his breast—the devout Christian, the earnest philanthropist, the enthusiastic athlete.

Significant in the formation of muscular Christianity were semi-biographical writings of Thomas Hughes, who wrote *Tom Brown's School Days* in 1857, and *Tom Brown at Oxford* in 1859. These books encouraged physical strength, health and strong moral principles.

As a youth, Thomas Hughes attended

Rugby School, located in the town of Rugby in Warwickshire, England. It was a public school free to all boys who lived within ten miles of the town's clock tower. The game of rugby was invented at the school.

The legend is, during a school soccer match in 1823, student Webb Ellis picked up the ball and ran with it. Today, the international Rugby World Cup gives the winner The Webb Ellis Trophy.

In America, the game of rugby developed into the game of football. Instead of players fighting for over the ball in a closely packed scrummage, they competed on a line of scrimmage.

The head master of Rugby School from 1828 to 1841, was Thomas Arnold. He was strict yet caring, resulting in the students holding him in respect and admiration. He was known for the force of his character and his firm faith.

As recorded in J.J. Findlay's *Arnold of Rugby: His School Life and Contributions to Education* (Cambridge University Press, 1897):

> The one thing needful for a Christian and an Englishman to study is: Christian and moral and political philosophy.

Arnold's educational reforms emphasized masculinity and achievement. He stated:

> First religious and moral principle, second gentlemanly conduct, third academic ability.

Other public schools copied his goals, which he prioritized as: the cure of souls, then moral development, followed by intellectual development.

Arthur Stanley wrote in *The Life and*

Correspondence of Thomas Arnold (London: 1844):

> His great object (was) ... making the school a place of really Christian education ... It was not an attempt merely to give more theological instruction ...
>
> "The business of a schoolmaster," he used to say," no less than that of a parish minister, is the cure of souls" ... The boys were ... treated as schoolboys ... who must grow up to be Christian men.

As recorded in *Thomas Arnold, Sermons Volumes 1 & II* (London: Longmans, Green & Co., 1878), Arnold stated:

> So many boys' souls are utterly lost in the worship and service of Satan ...
>
> Christ ... alone can give us a new and healthy nature; He alone can teach us so to live, as to make this world a school for heaven.

Princeton Professor James O. Murray wrote in his book *Francis Wayland*, by, 1891:

> Dr. Arnold, of Rugby, molded the religious thinking of his pupils, and so ultimately that of wide circles in England ... Dr. Arnold (declared) "It is not necessary that this should be a school of three hundred or one hundred or of fifty boys; but it is necessary that it should be a school of Christian gentlemen."

Arnold encouraged boys to play sports as an alternative to disorderly conduct and fighting. He taught that real men kept their feelings under control. To this end, sports were incorporated into Rugby School's curriculum. Since the game of Rugby took its name from the school, Arnold is considered the father of the sport of rugby.

In 1880, Thomas Hughes, author of *Tom Brown's School Days,* immigrated to the United States and founded the Christian community of Rugby, Tennessee, based on Arnold's values.

Fred Bailey, a retired history professor at Abilene Christian University, stated in a lecture at Oak Ridge Institute for Continued Learning (D. Ray Smith, *The Oakridger*, September 28, 2023):

> One volume always on display in the Thomas Hughes Public Library in Rugby, Tennessee, which is across from the chapel, is the children's book Hughes wrote entitled *Tom Brown's School Days*. It was an incredible little book because of its influence.
>
> The American president, Theodore Roosevelt, read it as a boy and said every boy should read it.

Arthur Penrhyn Stanley's *The life and correspondence of Thomas Arnold* (London: B. Fellowes, 1845), quotes a student describing Arnold:

> "He appeared to me," writes a pupil, "to be remarkable for his habit of realizing everything that we are told in Scripture ... He seemed to have the freshest view of our Lord's life and death that I ever knew a man to possess. His rich mind filled up the naked outline of the Gospel history; — it was to him the most interesting fact that has ever happened, — is real, as exciting (if I may use the expression) as any recent event in modern history of which the actual effects are visible." (I, 156).

In 1841, Thomas Arnold was appointed as Oxford University's Regius Professor of Modern History. His works, *History of Rome*, 1838–1842, and *Lectures on Modern History,* in addition to his five volumes of sermons, were read across Britain, including by Queen Victoria.

In a sermon to students in the chapel at Rugby School, published 1845, Thomas Arnold declared:

> I hold that the revival of the church of Christ in its full perfection, to be the one great end to which all our efforts should be directed.

Muscular Christianity is summarized in 6 points:

1) a man's body is given to him by God;
2) and to be trained;
3) and brought into subjection;
4) and then used for the protection of the weak;
5) for the advancement of all righteous causes;
6) and for the subduing of the earth which God has given to the children of men.

Thomas Hughes wrote in *Tom Brown at Oxford*, 1859:

> It is a good thing to have strong and well-exercised bodies ... The least of the muscular Christians have hold of the old chivalrous and Christian belief, that a man's body is given him to be trained and brought into subjection, and then used for the protection of the weak, the advancement of all righteous causes, and the subduing of the earth which God has given to the children of men.

ST. PAUL'S ATHLETIC METAPHORS

Muscular Christianity is inspired by the Apostle Paul's athletic metaphors describing how to be victorious in the challenges of life.

"Train yourself for godliness." 1 Timothy 4:7. The Greek word for train is gymnazō, which is a reference to exercise.

"Be a good servant of Christ Jesus, being trained in the words of the faith." 1 Timothy 4:6

"I discipline my body and keep it under control, lest after preaching to others I myself should be disqualified." I Corinthians 9:27. The Greek word for "discipline" is hupopiazō, which means "to bruise, to beat black and blue."

"Every athlete exercises self-control in all things." 1 Corinthians 9:25.

"An athlete is not crowned unless he competes according to the rules" 2 Timothy 2:5.

"To this end we labor and strive, because we have our hope set on the living God." 1 Timothy 4:10. The Greek word for "labor," kopiaō, means "to toil to the point of exhaustion."

"Not that I have already obtained all this, or have already arrived at my goal, but I press on to take hold of that for which Christ

Jesus took hold of me." Philippians 3:12. The Greek word for "press" is diokō, which means "to move rapidly and decisively after an object."

"Let us run with endurance, the race that is set before us." Hebrews 12:1. The Greek word for "race" is agōn, which is an exhausting long-distance event.

David J. Williams described in *Paul's Metaphors: Their Context and Character* (Hendrickson, 1999) that the Bible verse in Galatians 5:7 "You were running well. Who hindered you from obeying the truth?" (ESV) was a reference to a runner being cut off or tripped by another runner, as in the Greek Olympic race:

> The Greek stadium was a rectangle about 220 yards long by 8 to 13 yards wide.
>
> A line at each end marked the start and the finish, and there was a turning post in the middle of each line. In races longer than a single lap, the runners had to circle the post.
>
> This presented less of a problem in the dolichos (the long race). But in the diaulos, which was only two laps run at full speed, the turn was of critical importance.
>
> When the runners were of comparable ability, bunching at the post was inevitable and interference was likely to occur ...
>
> In terms of Paul's metaphor, it was at this point that the Galatians had run into trouble.

Paul also stated:

> "I do not consider myself yet to have taken hold of it. But one thing I do: Forgetting what is behind and straining

toward what is ahead." Philippians 3:13.

"Do you not know that in a race all the runners run, but only one gets the prize? Run in such a way as to get the prize." 1 Corinthians 9:24

"I do not run like someone who doesn't run toward the finish line. I do not fight like a boxer who hits nothing but air." I Corinthians 9:26 NIRV.

"Fight the good fight of faith." 1 Timothy 6:12

"I have fought the good fight, I have finished the race, I have kept the faith." 2 Timothy 4:7.

◦⁀◦

OLYMPIC GAMES REVIVED

In 1883, 20-year-old Frenchman Charles Pierre de Frédy, Baron de Coubertin, visited England's Rugby School. He studied Thomas Arnold's program of physical education.

Rugby School, as depicted in *Tom Brown's School Days*, 1857, led de Coubertin to write:

> Thomas Arnold, the leader and classic model of English educators gave the precise formula for the role of athletics in education. The cause was quickly won. Playing fields sprang up all over England.

De Coubertin traveled England to observe how Arnold's model influenced schools all across the nation, as described in his book *L'Education en Angleterre,* published in Paris in 1888. He recommended French schools adopt Arnold's example and add sports to their curriculum.

On his second visit to Rugby School in 1886, de Coubertin described sitting in the chapel and pondering the character–reforming influence of school boys playing sports, and concluded that "organized sport can create moral and social strength." It kept boys from wasting time and produced equilibrium in mind and body.

De Coubertin considered Arnold as "one of the founders of athletic chivalry," and credited Rugby's muscular Christianity as the reason the British Empire powerfully expanded in the 19th century. He recalled while looking at Arnold's tomb in the school chapel that he was looking at "the very cornerstone of the British empire."

De Coubertin was also aware of Y.M.C.A. chapters springing up around the world emphasizing athletics and organizing sports competitions.

All this resulted in de Coubertin broadening his vision. Not only should athletic competition be introduced into French schools, but into countries all around the world, and then those countries send athletes together, not in war, but in peace to compete in athletic competitions.

De Coubertin studied ancient Olympic games, begun in 776 B.C., in Olympia, Greece, and held every four years, called an Olympiad, until Emperor Theodosius ended them in 393 A.D.

De Coubertin conceived of the idea of bringing the ancient Olympic Games back. It took years of overcoming hurdles in international relations, especially between France and Germany, but finally his dream became a reality in 1896, when the Summer Olympic Games were held in Athens.

King George I of Greece wrote June 21, 1894:

> With deep feeling towards Baron de Coubertin's courteous petition, I send him and the members of the Congress ... my sincere thanks, my best wishes for the revival of the Olympic Games.

The Rugby School website gives the history. Rugbyschool.co.uk/about/history/:

> Arnold's ideas ... found particularly fertile ground ... in the mind of one French boy ... Pierre de Coubertin was twelve years old when he first encountered Thomas Arnold in the pages of *Tom Brown's School Days* ... The novel was translated into French in 1875 ...
>
> Inspired by what he had read, de Coubertin visited Rugby several times during the 1880s and concluded that organized sport could be used to raise the aspirations and improve the behavior of young people.
>
> This idea fueled his vision for universal amateur athletics which culminated, in 1896, in the first modern Olympic Games in Athens.
>
> As one world expert on Olympic history says, "Thomas Arnold was the single most important influence on the life and thought of Pierre de Coubertin."

Arnold's influential role in the Olympic Games is commemorated in a plaque on the School's Doctor's Wall, unveiled by Lord Sebastian Coe in 2009.

In July 2012 the Olympic Torch came to Rugby School on its route towards the Olympic Stadium and paused at the plaque to acknowledge the importance of Thomas Arnold who would certainly have enjoyed the school's re-enactment of a 19th century game of rugby with the boys wearing kilt of the time.

Y.M.C.A. SENT ATHLETES TO OLYMPICS

De Coubertin reached out to Y.M.C.A. director Elwood S. Brown for help recruiting athletes to compete in the Olympics. Brown, during the early 1900s, was the primary promoter of Muscular Christianity, Olympism, and the Protestant Work Ethic in East and Southeast Asia.

The Y.M.C.A. International website (accessed 1/18/25) stated:

> The relationship between the International Olympic Movement and the Young Men's Christian Association/ Y.M.C.A. dates back to the early days of modern Olympic Games ... when the institution played a meaningful role in the growth of this competition.
> Director of the Athletic Department

of the American Young Men's Christian Association, Elwood S. Brown, was paramount, who was very much involved in the organization of the games between the allies during World War I.

Elwood S. Brown graduated from Wheaton College, a school founded by Jonathan Blanchard modeled after Oberlin College, being evangelical Christian, abolitionist and open to all races. He coached at the University of Illinois Urbana–Champaign, was physical director at the Chicago Y.M.C.A., then at the Salt Lake City Y.M.C.A.

In 1910, Brown took the job of physical director at the Manila Y.M.C.A. chapter where he introduced basketball and volleyball. He founded the first Boy Scout troop in the Philippines.

When there was a great fire in Manila, he organized the Boy Scouts to be the first responders on the scene. Brown wrote of this to Theodore Roosevelt, who was at that time the honorary Vice-President of the Boy Scouts of America.

During World War I, Elwood Brown organized the American Expeditionary Force Games involving soldier athletes from many countries.

Baron de Coubertin took notice and contacted Brown. They agreed to partner together, using the infrastructure of Y.M.C.A. chapters worldwide to send athletes to compete in the Olympic games. Brown promoted Olympism to the Y.M.C.A.s in Latin America, India, and the Far East.

Y.M.C.A.s around the globe provided facilities for Olympic athletes to train. The first Olympic delegation from Argentina was coordinated by Y.M.C.A. officials.

For its contribution, the Y.M.C.A. received the Olympic Cup in 1920, especially because the Y.M.C.A.s part in the creation of basketball and volleyball. In 1929, the Y.M.C.A. received the Olympic Cup for its contribution to growing the Olympic movement internationally.

In 1924, Y.M.C.A. professor Federico Dickens directed the Argentine Olympic team. Y.M.C.A. members Otto Dietsch and Francisco Dova broke the South American record in the 800 meter competition. That same year, Chicago Y.M.C.A. member Johnny Weissmuller won three Olympic gold medals in swimming. He later became famous for his performance of Tarzan.

In 1932, Toronto Y.M.C.A. member Horacio Gwyne won a gold medal in boxing in the Bantamweight Class. In 1936, the Mexican Basketball Team was made up of players from Y.M.C.A.s in Mexico City and Chihuahua. Also in 1936, Y.M.C.A. members from Argentina ran on the 4×100 relay team.

In 1948, Delfo Cabrera, a member of Y.M.C.A. Argentina, won an Olympic medal. In 1972, Seifu Makonnen, a Y.M.C.A. member from Ethiopia, represented his country in Olympic boxing. In 1972, Mark Spitz, a member of the Y.M.C.A. Sacramento, won 7 gold medals in swimming.

Ian Crocker learned how to swim at the Portland, Oregon, Y.M.C.A. He competed in the 2000 and 2004 Olympic Games, winning four gold medals. Michael Phelps won a total of 28 Olympic medals, more than any other athlete, and went on to be a professor at the Baltimore County, Maryland, Y.M.C.A. Aquatics Center.

Originally, women did not compete in the Olympics, as de Coubertin viewed sports as a substitute for boys fighting at school and men fighting in battles. Gradually, women participated in Olympic competition, beginning in 1900 with golf and tennis; 1904 with archery; 1908 with figure skating; 1912 with swimming.

Alice Millet organized a separate Women's Olympiad in 1922, which included track and field, basketball, gymnastics, pushball and rhythmic gymnastics. These games continued until 1938, when they combined with the Olympic Games.

CHARIOTS OF FIRE

The award-winning film, *Chariots of Fire*, 1981, is about Scottish rugby player and sprinter Eric Liddell. Born in China to missionary parents, he was sent at age 6 to a boarding school in London. He attended the University of Edinburgh where he became known as the fastest runner in Scotland.

Calls arose for him to compete in the 1924 Olympics in Paris. The movie depicted his running coach pressing him, with Eric's brother, Robert, agreeing: "What we need now is a muscular Christian to make folks sit up and notice."

Reverend James Liddell, Eric's missionary father back from China, told him:

> Eric, you can praise the Lord by peeling a spud (potato) if you peel it to perfection. Don't compromise.

Compromise is the language of the devil. Run in God's name and let the world stand back and wonder.

His sister, Jennie, tried to get him to give up running to focus on church work, Eric answered, "I believe God made me for a purpose, but he also made me fast. And when I run I feel His pleasure."

When the Olympic schedule was published, Eric was disappointed to see his race, the 100-metre, set on a Sunday. Being a devout Christian, it was against his principle to work on the Sabbath, so he withdrew from the race.

The British Olympic committee, including the Prince of Wales, tried to convince him otherwise, but he would not. Fortunately, a teammate gave Liddell his place in the 400-metre race on a different day. The movie depicted the scene:

> Duke of Sutherland: "A sticky moment, George."
> Lord Birkenhead: "Thank God for Lindsay (the runner who gave up his place). I thought the lad (Liddell) had us beaten."
> Duke of Sutherland: "He did have us beaten, and thank God he did."
> Lord Birkenhead: "I don't quite follow you."
> Duke of Sutherland: "The 'lad,' as you call him, is a true man of principles and a true athlete. His speed is a mere extension of his life, its force. We sought to sever his running from himself."

Liddell spent months training for the 400-metre. On July 11, 1924, the morning of the Olympic 400-metre final, Liddell was handed a small piece of paper with a reference to I Samuel 2:30: "In the old book it says: 'He that honors me I will honor.'

Wishing you the best of success always."

Liddell drew the outside lane, which, due to the curve of the track, deprived him of seeing the other runners. Instead of pacing himself, as was normal in middle-distance races, he sprinted the entire race. He came around the final bend to win, breaking not just the Olympic record, but the world record, with a time of 47.6 seconds.

Not long after, Liddell returned to northern China to serve as a missionary from 1925 to 1943.

When the Japanese invaded, he was confined with others to an internment camp, which weakened his health before his death. Always ministering, a fellow internee, Norman Cliff, wrote in *The Courtyard of the Happy Way:*

> Liddell was the finest Christian gentleman it has been my pleasure to meet. In all the time in the camp, I never heard him say a bad word about anybody.

A survivor of the camp, Langdon Gilkey, wrote:

> Liddell was absorbed, weary and interested, pouring all of himself into this effort to capture the imagination of these penned-up youths. He was overflowing with good humor and love for life, and with enthusiasm and charm. It is rare indeed that a person has the good fortune to meet a saint, but he came as close to it as anyone I have ever known.

In 2002, he was inducted into the Scottish Sports Hall of Fame as Scotland's most popular sports hero. In 2022, he was inducted into the Scottish Rugby Hall of Fame.

Once asked if he regretted his decision to leave his fame to be a missionary, he responded:

> It's natural for a chap to think over all that sometimes, but I'm glad I'm at the work I'm engaged in now. A fellow's life counts for far more at this than the other.

᎗

SOME HISTORY OF ATHLETICS

Just as Thomas Arnold, in 1850, introduced organized sports at Rugby School as an alternative to school boys fighting, in like manner, Baron de Coubertin's vision was to introduce athletic competition between nations as an alternative to men fighting in wars.

This was attempting a major shift, as from time immemorial, nations have fought. Physical fitness was simply viewed as preparation for war.

Historically, athletics was to train for combat, by wrestling, boxing, weightlifting, and pankration – a type of mixed martial art with kicking and choking, javelin throwing, archery, swordsmanship, fencing, hatchet-throwing, long jumping, high jumping, bull-leaping, gymnastics, rowing, swimming, and foot racing.

The marathon foot race commemorates when a messenger ran from the Battle of Marathon to Athens, 490 B.C., to bring news of the Greek military victory over the Persians.

Another run after a battle was in I Samuel 4:

> Then a man of Benjamin ran from the battle line ... and came to Shiloh ... Now when he came, there was Eli, sitting on a seat by the wayside watching.

Absalom's defeat began a foot race, II Samuel 18:

> Then Ahimaaz the son of Zadok said, "Let me run now and take the news to the king, how the Lord has avenged him of his enemies."
>
> And Joab said to him, "You shall not take the news this day ... because the king's son is dead."
>
> Then Joab said to the Cushite, "Go, tell the king what you have seen." So the Cushite bowed himself to Joab and ran.
>
> And Ahimaaz the son of Zadok said again to Joab ... "Please let me also run after the Cushite."
>
> So Joab said, "Why will you run, my son, since you have no news ready?" ... "But ..." he said, "let me run."
>
> So he said to him, "Run." Then Ahimaaz ran by way of the plain, and outran the Cushite.

In other nations, athletic competition was a substitute for battle. Mayans had a Mesoamerican ballgame played with a 9 lb. solid rubber ball, as rubber originated in Mexico's Olmec region. The game, dating as early as 1650 B.C., was a proxy for warfare between tribes, with players even dressing as warriors.

The Mexican game was a mix of racquetball and soccer, with players using their hips to knock a hard rubber ball through a stone hoop. It was a violent game, with some players dying.

Gladiatorial games in Roman amphitheaters were a mix of martial arts and mortal combat. Warfare was continually on men's minds. Even hunting trips had aspects of military training.

Ancient board games were essentially mock battles. India's ancient military strategy game of Chaturanga, the Japanese game of Shogi, the Middle Eastern game of alquerque or checkers, the Roman game of Ludus Latrunculorum, the 4th century Scandinavia game of Tafl, the 13th century Medieval game of chess, and the Chinese strategy game of "Go."

In 776 B.C., the first Olympic Games were held in Greece. Athletes from different cities and countries competed in sprint and long distance runs. Wrestling was added next.

In the 6th century B.C., Greeks held Heraean games in Olympia, where women competed against women. The games were named after Hera, the Greek goddess representing marriage, women, family, and the protector of women during childbirth.

Some sports focused on teamwork so as to better function as a military unit in battle. During ancient India Vedic period, 1500 to 500 B.C., the game of Kabaddi was invented, a contact team sport with seven players on a side.

In 206 B.C., China's Han Dynasty had a kick ball game called cuju, with competitive fitness training being recorded in a military manual.

Ireland had a Gaelic team sport called "hurling," a mix of rugby, lacrosse and field hockey, dating from the 5th century. The Irish have tales of great hurling players, such as the legendary Táin Bó Cuailnge praising the warrior Cúchulainn hurling at Emain Macha.

In England, a team sport using sticks developed called cricket. Scotland's version of the game is called shinty. In the 15th century Scotland saw another game develop with sticks – golf.

With the invention of the stirrup in Mongolia, horses became essential in battle. The stirrup made its way over the China Silk Road to Persia.

In Persia, to practice for cavalry warfare, an equestrian sport with sticks developed in the 3rd century called Chovgan, which turned into polo, the sport of kings.

Byzantine Emperor Theodosius II encouraged horsemanship by constructing an enormous outdoor polo area in the 5th century. Polo became popular in Central Asia, India, Tibet, and China during the Tang Dynasty.

Due to the expense, only elites could afford to participate in equestrian sports, which included horse racing, chariot racing, horseback archery, and jousting.

In the 12th century, a type of racquetball developed using the palm of the hand, jeu de paume. King Louis X was a avid player, but, unfortunately, after playing an exhausting game in June of 1316, he quenched his thirst by consuming too much cooled wine and died.

In the 16th century, paddles and rackets were added to the game and it evolved into the royal sport of tennis. England's Henry VIII was a fan of tennis. In 1830, with the invention of lawnmowers, lawn tennis courts came into vogue with Europe's upper class.

Most sports were only for wealthy elites, as they could afford expensive equipment and had free time to practice. Occasionally, a well performing commoner could gain recognition through sports and rise in social standing.

Muscular Christianity as a movement broadened sports from the pastime of the elites, or preparation for combat, to a healthy activity the common man could participate in, improving physical ability and mental acuity, with lessons applicable to spiritual warfare.

The strength, discipline and self-control developed through athletics improved one's ability to carry out the will of God which included helping the weak, defending the defenseless, protecting the orphan and the widow, rescuing the innocent from injustice, and displaying self-sacrificing patriotism.

OBERLIN COLLEGE & THE ABOLITION MOVEMENT

Christians being strong and active against injustice preceded the Civil War, with a demand to end slavery immediately.

Oberlin College was described as an "academic powder keg of abolitionism," in Louis A. DeCaro Jr.'s book *"Fire from the Midst of You" – A Religious Life of John Brown* (New York University Press, 2002)

Oberlin College was founded as a result of Charles Finney's revival preaching. Oberlin alumni J.H. Fairchild explained in his address, August 22, 1860, "Oberlin was the offspring of the revivals of 1830, '31, and '32."

It began when the college's founder, 28-year-old John Jay Shipherd, was traveling on his first business trip through Western New York to Ohio. That was at the time Finney was preaching.

Shipherd heard Finney and was so inspired he sought him out. He requested a meeting in Rochester. Afterwards, Finney was so impressed with Shipherd's desire to spread Christianity that he offered him a job as his assistant.

Though honored, Shipherd declined, as Geoffrey Blodgett explained in *Oberlin History. Essays and Impressions* (Kent State University Press, 2006):

> Shipherd ... felt that he had his own important part to play in bringing on the millennium, God's triumphant reign on Earth. Finney's desires were one thing, but Shipherd believed that the Lord's work for him lay farther west.

In 1833, Shipherd and Presbyterian minister Philo Steward, a missionary among the Cherokee in Mississippi, founded Oberlin Collegiate Institute to train ministers and missionaries.

They named it after the French minister Jean-Frédéric Oberlin who introduced into the Alsace region of eastern France the teaching that Christian's should not be spectators but involved. His teachings were described as the "true precursor of social Christianity in France."

His views were akin to Benjamin Franklin's, that one's faith should effect society for the good. Franklin wrote to Joseph Huey, June 6, 1753:

> The worship of God is a duty; the hearing and reading of sermons may be useful; but, if men rest in hearing and praying, as too many do, it is as if a tree should value itself on being watered and putting forth leaves, though it never produce any fruit.

Franklin wrote in his *Autobiography* of the Presbyterian minister in Philadelphia:

> He used to visit me ... and admonish me to attend ... I was now and then prevailed on to do so, once for five Sundays successively.
>
> Had he been in my opinion a good preacher, perhaps I might have continued ... but his discourses were chiefly either polemic arguments, or explications of the peculiar doctrines of our sect, and were all to me very dry, uninteresting, and unedifying ... and I attended his preaching no more.

John Morgan graduated valedictorian from Williams College in 1826, and became a Latin instructor at Lane Theological School in Cincinnati, Ohio. A faculty member, he sponsored a student-led anti-slavery society.

Disgruntled trustees fired Morgan, over the opposition of school president Lyman Beecher, and benefactors, wealthy silk importer brothers Arthur and Lewis Tappan. Arthur was president of the American anti-slavery society, and Lewis was a delegate to the World Anti-slavery Convention. The students who withdrew from Lane attended Oberlin, which also hired John Morgan.

Oberlin College enrolled young men, and beginning in 1837, accepted the first women students, being the oldest "co-educational" liberal arts college in the U.S. and the second-oldest continuously operating "co-educational" institute of higher learning in the world.

Herbert Galen Lull described in *The Manual Labor Movement In the United States*, June 1914, that the school vision was to be a community of Christian families with a school teaching "practical theology":

> ... a center of religious influence and power which should work mightily upon the surrounding country and the world—a sort of missionary institution for training laborers for the work abroad.

Students were required to sign the Oberlin Covenant to maintain plain, straight living, no smoking, no tobacco chewing, no coffee or tea, no tight dresses, or fancy houses, furniture, and carriages, with the main thrust being missionary education to save a perishing world.

Shipherd wrote:

> Each member of the colony shall consider himself a steward of the Lord, and ... return to Gospel simplicity ... to glorify God in the salvation of men.

Oberlin was strongly anti-slavery, promoting "immediatism," that is, demanding immediate freedom for slaves.

J. Brent Morris wrote in *Oberlin, Hotbed of Abolitionism: College, Community, and the Fight for Freedom and Equality in Antebellum America*

(University of North Carolina Press, 2014) that it was founded for the purpose of

> ... educating a missionary army of Christian soldiers to save the world and inaugurate God's government on earth, and the radical notion that slavery was America's most horrendous sin that should be instantly repented of and immediately brought to an end.

Pro-slavery southern Democrats were content with the status quo. They were threatened by Oberlin's growing influence and attempted to counter it by twisting Scriptures to shame Christians into not being involved in politics.

Anti-slavery philanthropist brothers, Lewis and Arthur Tappan, supported Oberlin College.

In 1835, Shipherd persuaded Charles Finney to begin teaching at Oberlin College. Finney became the second president, serving from 1851 to 1865.

Under Finney, the college was one of the first in the nation to admit African–American students. In 1862, Oberlin graduated Mary Jane Patterson, the first black woman to graduate from a college in the United States.

Oberlin's campus was part of the Underground Railroad, smuggling slaves to freedom. Its students became what were called "radical Republicans," traveling to southern Democrat states preaching "immediatism," that slaves should be freed immediately.

Oberlin trustees passed, February 1835:

> That the education of the people of color is a matter of great interest and

should be encouraged and sustained in this Institution.

Articles from Oberlin faculty were published in the abolitionist newspaper *The Liberator.*

In 1839, abolitionist pastor Jonathan Blanchard delivered a commencement address at Oberlin College. There he witnessed the work of the Holy Spirit in staff and students. Blanchard became president of Knox College in Galesburg, Illinois, founded by George W. Gale, who had been Charles Finney's pastor in Adams, New York. Blanchard became president of Wheaton College in 1882.

Wheaton College's 4th president, V. Raymond Edman, wrote *Finney Lives On: The Secret of Revival in Our Time*, 1951. Billy Graham described it, "To read, study and pray over this book is an imperative for every Christian worker in such an hour as this." Raymond Edman wrote:

> Thus was Charles Grandison Finney, the lad who grew up in the backwoods of America without any knowledge of the gospel, the young lawyer who met the Lord Jesus in true penitence and prayer, the man who was devoted to the Scriptures and the Savior, the revivalist whose tireless labors shook America and Britain in decades that were dark with human greed and godlessness, the pastor and college president whose ministry led multitudes to the Master and sent them to the ends of the earth in His glad service, the servant of Christ who still lives in Christian hearts the world over as he thunders to us in his *Memoirs, Lectures on Revivals of Religion*, and *Lectures to Professing Christians.*

Since Oberlin trained ministers and missionaries, it realized the importance of singing Gospel music prior to preaching, so the school had a choir program.

Rev. Elihu Parsons Ingersoll was Oberlin's professor of Sacred Music, the first-ever professor of music at an American college. He was a great-grandson of Jonathan Edwards, the New England pastor of the First Great Awakening Revival.

Ingersoll was followed by George N. Allen, who was inspired by composer Felix Mendelssohn, renown for composing the music for Charles Wesley's Christmas carol, "Hark! the Herald Angels Sing." Mendelssohn founded the Leipzig Conservatory of Music in Germany, in 1843.

George Allen followed his example and formed Oberlin Musical Union in 1865, renamed Oberlin Conservatory of Music, the oldest continuously operating music conservatory in America.

LAYMAN'S PRAYER REVIVAL

In 1844, the world faced many challenges. A New England farmer, William Miller, seized national attention by predicting Christ would return on October 22, 1844, and set up his millennium kingdom. When it did not occur, many abandoned their faith in what was called The Millerite Great Disappointment.

The Mexican–America War began in 1846, and ended in 1848.

In 1849, gold was discovered in California.

The same year, a cholera epidemic swept the nation, killing 150,000. President Zachary Taylor proclaimed a National Day of Fasting, and shortly thereafter the pandemic ended.

At this time, the Democrat-controlled Congress pushed through the Compromise of 1850 and the Fugitive Slave Law, which intensified the conflict of slavery. In 1851, Harriet Beecher Stowe published her anti-slavery novel *Uncle Tom's Cabin*. That same year Herman Melville published his whaling novel, *Moby Dick*.

In 1853, James Gadsden, the U.S. Minister to Mexico, negotiated the United States giving $10 million to General Antonio López de Santa Anna in exchange for the Gadsden Purchase. This allowed railroads from the east to connect to the Pacific coast, forever changing the old wild west.

Democrats wanted the western territories to come into the Union as slave states. In 1854, Democrat Senator from Illinois Stephen Douglas pushed through the Kansas–Nebraska Act, which prompted a flood of pro-slavery Democrats to move west, so as to have those territories come into the Union as slave states. This caused the pre-Civil War conflict called "bleeding Kansas."

In 1854, the slave Joshua Glover escaped from St. Louis, Missouri, and fled to Racine, Wisconsin. The St. Louis sheriff, authorized by the Fugitive Slave Law, went to Racine and captured Joshua Glover and put in the Milwaukee jail.

On March 18, 1854, five thousand Wisconsin citizens stormed the Milwaukee jail, freed Joshua Glover, and shortly after, formed a political party dedicated to end slavery – the Republican Party.

In 1855, escaped slave Frederick Douglass, a Republican, published his autobiography *My Bondage–My Freedom.*

In 1856, Wesleyan Methodist minister William Arthur printed a soul-stirring book of sermons, *The Tongue of Fire, or true Power of Christianity.*

The book was endorsed by the renown preacher Charles Spurgeon of London's Metropolitan Tabernacle. Spurgeon wrote:

> I know of no better thermometer to your spiritual temperature than this, the measure of the intensity of your prayer ... Oh, my brethren! bold-hearted men are always called mean-spirited by cowards ...
>
> I believe the holier a man becomes, the more he mourns over the unholiness which remains in him

The last chapter of William Arthur's book ended with a plea that God would:

> ... crown this nineteenth century with a revival of pure and undefiled religion ... greater than any demonstration of the Spirit ever vouchsafed to man.

Arthur's book had an impact similar to Charles Finney's *Lectures on Revivals of Religion.*

In 1857, a financial panic hit America, the third since the nation's founding. Banks failed, railroads went bankrupt, factories closed, and in New York, over 900 mercantile firms went out of business leaving over 30,000 out of work.

Even a St. Louis farmer and former army captain, Ulysses S. Grant, had to pawn his gold watch.

In this crisis, Jeremiah Lamphier began a

prayer meeting in New York. Converted in 1842 at age 33, while visiting Charles Finney's Broadway Tabernacle, Lamphier was a businessman who became a lay missionary with the Dutch Reformed North Church near Fulton and William Streets.

He put a sign in front of his store, inviting merchants, clerks, mechanics and others, to join him for noonday prayer for one hour on Wednesdays. The first meeting, September 23, 1857, only six showed up. The next week 40.

They decided to pray daily, and within six months, there were ten thousand participating in the Layman's Prayer Revival. Spreading across the nation, a million converts prayed day and night in the next two years. Many of these prayer meetings were held in Y.M.C.A. buildings.

Vice and crime decreased, criminals returned stolen money, wealthy helped the poor, salty sailors prayed openly, and when ungodly shipmates mocked them, the presence of God caused them to kneel in repentance.

A religious journal reported in March of 1858:

> The large cities and towns from Maine to California are sharing in this great and glorious work. There is hardly a village or town to be found where "a special divine power" does not appear displayed.

Run by lay leadership, the revival spread:

> New York City – 50,000 of the city's 800,000 population became new converts;
> Utica, New York – daily prayer meetings filled the First Presbyterian Church, overflowing the balconies;
> Albany, New York – the State Capitol

had prayer in the halls every morning beginning at 8:30am;

Newark, New Jersey – 3,000 came to Christ, with nearby towns seeing almost their entire populations converted;

Boston, Massachusetts – businessmen and commoners attended together, as a witness recorded, "Publicans and sinners" are awakened, and are entering the prayer meetings of their own accord. Some of them manifest signs of sincere repentance;

Haverhill, Massachusetts – crowds came daily, weeping in repentance. Every family had someone seeking God;

Washington, DC – prayer meetings were held five times a day to accommodate the scores of seekers;

Philadelphia, Pennsylvania – 4,000 met in Jayne's Hall, as witnessed by philanthropist John Price Crozer, "I have never, I think, been present at a more stirring and edifying prayer meeting, the room quite full, and a divine influence seemed manifest. Many hearts melted, many souls devoutly engaged";

Pittsburgh, Pennsylvania – 6,000 attended prayer meetings;

Kalamazoo, Michigan – a woman wrote a prayer request to be read publicly at the meeting for her husband's salvation. When it was read, a man shouted, "Pray for me. I'm that man";

Charleston, South Carolina – 2,000 prayed at Anson Street Presbyterian Church for 8 weeks. One night, Dr. John L. Giradeaux dismissed the meeting, but no one left, staying till past midnight.

Waco, Texas – as reported in *The New York Observer*, "Day and night the church has been crowded during the meeting... Never before in Texas have we seen a whole community so effectually under a religious influence ... thoroughly regenerated";

Louisville, Kentucky – 1,000 attended the daily union prayer, as one witness wrote, "The Spirit of God seems to be brooding over our city, and to have produced an unusual degree of tenderness and solemnity in all classes";

Chicago, Illinois – 2,000 met for noon prayer at the Metropolitan Hall, with a sign reading, "Will reopen at the close of the prayer meeting."

Professor J. Edwin Orr of Fuller Theological Seminary estimated that the 1858–1859 Layman's Prayer Revival resulted in an increase in church attendance, moral reform in society, and over a million Americans converting to faith in Christ.

The Layman's Prayer Revival fanned the abolitionist movement and the Protestant social gospel movement to "civilize and Christianize" the world through charitable activities.

Y.M.C.A. WEEK OF PRAYER

Since many of the Layman's Prayer Revival meetings were held at Y.M.C.A. buildings, the Y.M.C.A. organization decided to sponsor an annual Week of Prayer.

The World Y.M.C.A.'s webpage "History of

the Week of Prayer" (accessed 1/14/25) gives the background. In a letter to the London Y.M.C.A. in 1856, F.R. Starr of Philadelphia suggested:

> The appointment of a week to be simultaneously observed by the Young Men's Christian Associations throughout the world for prayer for the conversion of the world, and for young men especially.

At the 5th Y.M.C.A. World Conference in Paris in 1867, the American delegation proposed that the second Sunday in November begin a week of prayer for all associations throughout the world.

At the 7th World Conference in Hamburg, 1875, the Y.M.C.A. agreed that every year, the second Sunday of November would be a "Week of Prayer. In 1891, the World Alliance of Y.M.C.A.s included the "Week of Prayer" in its Constitution.

RESCUE THOSE IN NEED

Muscular Christianity embodies the Scriptures dealing with mankind being given authority over the earth as stewards, and to use God's blessing to advance His Kingdom:

> "Then the LORD God took the man and put him in the Garden of Eden to cultivate it and tend it." Genesis 2:15

> "God said unto them, 'Be fruitful and multiply, and replenish the earth,

and subdue it; and have dominion over the fish of the sea, and over the fowl of the air, and over every living thing that moveth upon the earth.'" Genesis 1:28

"And God blessed Noah and his sons, and said unto them, 'Be fruitful, and multiply, and replenish the earth. And the fear of you and the dread of you shall be upon every beast of the earth ... into your hand are they delivered ... Bring forth abundantly in the earth, and multiply therein." Genesis 9:1–7

This differs from an early teaching of Gnostism, that the physical world was inherently evil and that one had to escape it by completely withdrawing, following secret knowledge, "gnosis," to attain a higher level of personal spirituality.

A version of this called asceticism, shaped classical antiquity – period of the 5th century to the early Middle Ages. Asceticism considered the flesh as a distraction from divinity, and that a person was holier if they neglected their body.

To some, this view produced a disconnected apathy regarding the condition of the world, preferring to withdraw and hide oneself in the solitude to a cave as a hermit, or cloister in a monastery, or take vows of poverty and silence.

This non-involvement perspective was a factor in Christianity being wiped out of North Africa by the Umayyad Muslim warriors, 661-743, as Christians were too withdrawn to offer resistance.

In contrast, Muscular Christianity emphasized courage and strength to carry out a righteous cause:

"Moses ... said to Joshua in the presence of all Israel, Be strong and courageous, for you must go with this people into the land that the Lord swore to their ancestors to give them, and you must divide it among them as their inheritance." Deuteronomy 31:7

"The Lord gave this command to Joshua ... 'Be strong and courageous, for you will bring the Israelites into the land I promised them on oath, and I myself will be with you.'" Deuteronomy 31:23

"Be strong and courageous, because you will lead these people to inherit the land I swore to their ancestors to give them." Joshua 1:6

"Be strong and very courageous. Be careful to obey all the law my servant Moses gave you; do not turn from it to the right or to the left, that you may be successful wherever you go." Joshua 1:7

"Be strong and courageous. Do not be afraid; do not be discouraged, for the Lord your God will be with you wherever you go." Joshua 1:9

"Only be strong and courageous!" Joshua 1:18

"Joshua said to them, 'Do not be afraid; do not be discouraged. Be strong and courageous. This is what the Lord will do to all the enemies you are going to fight.'" Joshua 10:25

"So we labored in the work, and half of the men held the spears from daybreak until the stars appeared." (Nehemiah 4:21)

God wants to bless His people so they can be a blessing to those in need:

"Now the Lord said unto Abram ... 'I will make you into a great nation, and I will bless you; I will make your name great, and you will be a blessing. I will bless those who bless you, and whoever curses you, I will curse; and all peoples on earth will be blessed through you.'" Genesis 12:2–3

God's people should care for those in need:

"Thou shalt not see thy brother's ox or his sheep go astray, and hide thyself from them: thou shalt in any case bring them again unto thy brother ... Thou shalt not see thy brother's ass or his ox fall down by the way, and hide thyself from them: thou shalt surely help him to lift them up again." Deuteronomy 22:1–4

Believers are to use their strength to help the weak.

"Rescue those who are unjustly sentenced to death; do not stand back and let them die. Do not try to disclaim responsibility by saying you did not know about it." Proverbs 24:11–12

"Rebuke the oppressor, obtain justice for the orphan, plead for the widow's case." Isaiah 1:17

"If you now remain silent, relief and deliverance will come to the Jews from another source; but you and your father's house will perish. Who knows — perhaps it was for a time like this that you became queen?" Esther 4:14

Believers are to have a heart of compassion:

"If a brother or sister be naked, and destitute of daily food, And one of you say unto them, Depart in peace, be ye warmed and filled; notwithstanding ye give them not those things which are needful to the body; what doth it profit?" James 2:15–16

"But whoso hath this world's goods and seeth his brother have need, and shutteth up the compassion of his heart from him, how dwelleth the love of God in him?" I John 3:17

Y.M.C.A.'S HENRI DUNANT FOUNDED RED CROSS

At the same time America was experiencing the Second Great Awakening Revival, a revival broke out in 1814 in western Switzerland and southeastern France called "La Réveil," through the Swiss Reformed Church. After Napoleon's fall from power, it was begun by Pietist Lutheran Moravian missionaries, aided by British Presbyterian Robert Haldane, Methodist Charles Cook, and members of the Free Church of Scotland.

Into this setting was born Henri Dunant in 1828, to a Calvinist family in Geneva, Switzerland.

At the age of 18, Henri joined the Geneva Society for Almsgiving, a Christian ministry to aid the less fortunate. He and his friends formed the "Thursday Association" to study the Bible and help the poor. His free time was occupied in social work and prison visits.

Dunant dropped out of the Collège de Genève due to low grades. At age 21, in 1849, he apprenticed at a money-changing firm, Lullin et Sautter. There he heard about the Y.M.C.A.

On November 30, 1852, Dunant founded the Geneva chapter of the Y.M.C.A. Martin Gumpert's *Dunant, The Story of the Red Cross* (NY: Oxford University Press, 1938, p. 22), recorded Henri Dunant stating:

> A group of Christian young men has met together in Geneva to do reverence and worship to the Lord Jesus whom they wish to serve ...
>
> They have heard that among you, too, there are brothers in Christ, young like themselves, who love their Redeemer and gather together that under His guidance, and through the reading of the Holy Scriptures, they may instruct themselves further.
>
> Being deeply edified thereby, they wish to unite with you in Christian friendship.

Dunant convinced the Paris Y.M.C.A. to host the first Y.M.C.A. World Conference in 1855, just 11 years after George Williams had the first meeting. 99 young delegates from 9 countries came. There they officially formed the

International Y.M.C.A., writing:

> Our object is the improvement of the spiritual condition of the young men engaged in houses of business, by the formation of Bible classes, family and social prayer meetings, mutual improvement societies, or any other spiritual agency.

Clyde Binfield recorded in *George Williams and the YMCA: A Study in Victorian Social Attitudes*, 1973, that delegates organized the International Y.M.C.A. for the purpose of:

> Christian discipleship developed through a program of religious, educational, social and physical activities," with the motto being the Bible verse, John 17:21, "That they all may be one."

Dunant enthusiastically promoted the founding of Y.M.C.A. chapters around the world, first across Europe and then in North Africa. He corresponded with leaders of chapters in over 30 cities, encouraging them and updating them on each other's growth.

Then the Battle of Solferino occurred in 1859 in northern Italy. Napoleon III's French army and Victor Emanuel II's Italian Piedmont–Sardinian army joined together in fighting against the Austrian army of Emperor Franz Joseph I.

Nearly 10,000 were killed and 23,000 wounded. After the battle, Dunant walked the battlefield and heard the cries of the wounded. This experience so moved him that he conceived the idea of organizing volunteers to care for battlefield wounded regardless of whose side they were on.

In 1863, at age 35, he founded the International Red Cross, for which he became the first recipient of the Nobel Peace Prize. In 1864, Dunant took part in the First Geneva Convention for the Amelioration of the Condition of the Wounded in Armies in the Field

In 1877–1878, when the Russo–Turkish War broke out, Dunant had the Red Cross operate under the name Red Crescent to allow Christian-motivated charity and humanitarian work to be carried on in Islamic countries. That symbol has since been recognized in 33 Islamic States.

The International Red Cross has since grown to aid 160 million people annually in 192 countries.

In 1897, Dunant supported Jews in their effort to repopulate their traditional homeland in Palestine. This was based on the Second Great Awakening teaching that before the prophecies of Christ's return to set up His millennial Kingdom can take place, Jews must be in possession of their ancient homeland.

Anita Shapira, *Israel a History* (Weidenfeld & Nicolson, 2014):

> The idea of the Jews returning to their ancient homeland as the first step to world redemption seems to have originated among a specific group of evangelical English Protestants that flourished in England in the 1840s; they passed this notion onto Jewish circles.

Geoffrey Alderman wrote in the *Jewish Chronicle*, November 8, 2012:

> The Balfour Declaration was born out

of religious sentiment. Arthur Balfour was a Christian mystic who believed that the Almighty had chosen him to be an instrument of the Divine Will, the purpose of which was to restore the Jews to their ancient homeland — perhaps as a precursor to the Second Coming of the Messiah. The Declaration was thus intended to assist in the fulfillment of biblical prophecy. This appealed to Lloyd George ... believing in the prophecies of a Bible he knew inside out.

Dunant was one of the few non-Jews to attend the First Zionist Congress in Basel, Switzerland, organized by Theodore Herzl. Herzl first used the term, "Christian Zionist" in reference to Dunant.

Dunant's Geneva Y.M.C.A. chapter became so influential that the decision was made to locate the Y.M.C.A.'s international headquarters there.

During the Franco–German War, 1870–1871, Clara Barton traveled to Europe to assist Dunant's International Red Cross in caring for the wounded. Afterwards, she returned to the U.S. to establish the American Red Cross Society, May 21, 1881.

CLARA BARTON FOUNDED AMERICAN RED CROSS

At age ten, Clara Barton saw her older brother, David, fall off the roof of a barn during barn-raising in Massachusetts.

Though the doctors gave up hope, Clara helped nurse him back to a full recovery. He became a Captain and served as Assistant Quartermaster for the Union Army during the Civil War.

In 1839, at the age of 17, Clara earned her teacher's certificate and taught for 12 years in Canada and West Georgia. In 1852, she moved to Bordertown, New Jersey, where she opened the state's first free school, and grew it to over 600 students.

In 1855, Clara moved to Washington, D.C., where she was hired as the first woman clerk at the U.S. Patent Office.

Democrat President James Buchanan's administration fired her because of her "Black Republicanism" – the Republican Party being the first party in history to have abolition of slavery in its party platform.

When Republican President Abraham Lincoln was elected, Clara was rehired at the U.S. Patent Office as a copyist.

When the Civil War began, the first blood was shed in a Baltimore riot, April 19, 1861. Forty wounded Union soldiers of the 6th Massachusetts Militia were brought by train to Washington, DC.. They were transported to a makeshift medical unit in the unfinished Capitol building.

Clara volunteered to care for them, recognizing many from her home state, some even having been her students. She worked with Ladies' Aid societies to collect and distribute medical supplies to wounded soldiers.

Ladies Christian Committees of the Y.M.C.A. were formed in every state affected by the war.

In 1862, Clara received permission to work with the Army on the front lines. Her patriotism came from her father, who served in the Army under General "Mad Anthony" Wayne. She wrote of helping soldiers:

> What could I do but go with them, or work for them and my country? The patriot blood of my father was warm in my veins.

She later wrote:

> I may be compelled to face danger, but never fear it, and while our soldiers can stand and fight, I can stand and feed and nurse them. I am well and strong and young – young enough to go to the front. If I cannot be a soldier, I'll help soldiers.

After working with Henri Dunant's International Red Cross in Europe, Clara Barton founded the American Red Cross Society on May 21, 1881.

Y.M.C.A. DURING CIVIL WAR

The Y.M.C.A. provided relief to soldiers during the Civil War through the U.S. Christian Commission, led by George Hay Stuart, founder of the Philadelphia Y.M.C.A. It was the nation's first large-scale civilian volunteer service corps.

Lincoln asked for 5,000 volunteers, writing to Stuart, December 12, 1861, that the "benevolent undertaking for the benefit of the soldiers" was "proper and praiseworthy," concluding:

"I sincerely hope your plan may be as successful in execution, as it is just and generous in conception."

The Armed Services Y.M.C.A. website (ASYMCA.org/about/history, accessed 1/14/25) tells of U.S. Christian Commission volunteers caring for sick and wounded soldiers in military encampments near the front lines.

They raised millions of dollars in private donations for supplies, hospital stores and clothing. Horse-drawn Y.M.C.A. canteens, called Coffee Wagons or Cooking Wagons, were in every camp, providing soldiers with an estimated 90 gallons an hour of tea, coffee or hot chocolate.

Y.M.C.A. volunteers staffed hospitals, set up prefabricated chapels, and engaged in prisoner-of-war efforts, ministering to the needs of both Confederate and Union soldiers. They distributed a hundred thousand cases of food, clothing, and medical supplies, along with 12 million books, magazines, a million Bibles, and 30 million Gospel tracts and New Testaments.

Volunteers wrote some 90,000 letters for the sick and wounded, and taught the illiterate to read.

George Hay Stuart personally gave a Bible to President Lincoln and to Ulysses Grant, writing:

> I have prayed for this Union; and I have labored for it, simply because I believed that it would bring glory to my blessed Lord and Master, Jesus Christ ... (and) because it would bring brethren together, now unhappily divided, to see eye to eye, that the nations that have so long bowed down to idols might learn of Jesus and Him

crucified ...

Since these twenty-four hours have passed away eighty-six thousand four hundred immortal souls have gone to the judgment seat of Christ ...

I never hear the funeral bell toll without asking myself the question, "What have I done to point that departed soul to the Lamb of God that died to save a perishing world?"

Brethren, buckle on your armor for a great conflict; buckle it on for giving the glorious Gospel of the Son of God to the millions of the earth who are perishing for lack of knowledge.

DWIGHT L. MOODY & THE CHICAGO Y.M.C.A.

Volunteers working the Y.M.C.A.'s U.S. Christian Commission included Walt Whitman and Dwight Lyman Moody.

Moody was born February 5, 1837. His father died when he was four, causing him to begin early earning money to support his family. He never finished his education.

Raised a unitarian, he was converted to evangelical Christianity in 1855 by his Sunday school teacher, Edward Kimball. Moody's *Memoirs* shared Kimball's initial opinion of Moody:

> I can truly say, and in saying it I magnify the infinite grace of God as bestowed upon

him, that I have seen few persons whose minds were spiritually darker than was his when he came into my Sunday School class;

and I think that the committee of the Mount Vernon Church seldom met an applicant for membership more unlikely ever to become a Christian of clear and decided views of Gospel truth, still less to fill any extended sphere of public usefulness.

Moody applied to be received as a church member, but the elders were unsure, hesitating to grant him membership until May 4, 1856.

He worked as a traveling shoe salesman for the Wiswall Brothers and was in Chicago during the Layman's Prayer Revival.

At the age of 21, Moody volunteered at the Y.M.C.A., serving anywhere there was a need, including janitorial jobs. He saw an abandoned saloon and began teaching a Sunday School mission there for underprivileged and immigrant children in inner city Chicago.

William Reynolds wrote of Moody's class:

> The first meeting I ever saw him at was in a little old shanty that had been abandoned by a saloon-keeper. Mr. Moody had got the place to hold the meetings in at night.
>
> I went there a little late; and the first thing I saw was a man standing up with a few tallow candles around him, holding a negro boy, and trying to read to him the story of the Prodigal Son and a great many words he could not read out, and had to skip.
>
> I thought, "If the Lord can ever use

such an instrument as that for His honor and glory, it will astonish me."

After that meeting was over, Mr. Moody said to me, "Reynolds, I have got only one talent: I have no education, but I love the Lord Jesus Christ, and I want to do something for him, and I want you to pray for me."

Moody stated:

> It is a masterpiece of the devil to make us believe that children cannot understand religion. Would Christ have made a child the standard of faith if He had known that it was not capable of understanding His words?

Moody was gifted in his ability to find capable people and put them into leadership. Within a year, he had 60 volunteers from different churches teaching over 650 children in his Sunday school.

By 1860, Moody's Chicago Bible class had grown to over 1,000 attendees. He began to work full time with the Y.M.C.A. as a "city missionary," though they could not afford to pay him.

Word of his class spread. Even President-elect Lincoln visited on his way through Chicago to Washington, DC., November 25, 1860. At Moody's prompting, Lincoln told the students:

> I was once as poor as any boy in this school, but I am now President of the United States, and if you attend to what is taught you here, some of you may yet be President of the United States.

A few years later, Lincoln was presented with

a Bible by a Colored Delegation from Baltimore. He responded, September 7, 1864:

> In regard to this Great Book, I have but to say, it is the best gift God has given to men ... But for it we could not know right from wrong.

When the Civil War began in 1861, D.L. Moody joined the Y.M.C.A.'s United States Christian Commission to minister to soldiers, praying for them and giving them Bibles.

He formed the Committee on Devotional Meetings for the 72nd Illinois Volunteer Regiment, located at Camp Douglas.

Nine times Moody was at the front lines, including the Battle of Shiloh, Battle of Stones River, and was with General Grant's troops when they entered Richmond, Virginia.

Moody's Mission Sunday School classes increased, resulting in attendees encouraging him to start the Illinois Street Church. The first service was February 28, 1864.

After the war, Moody served as president of the Chicago Y.M.C.A. from 1865–1870. At this time in history, Chicago was the second biggest city in America, after New York.

He married Emma C. Revell, August 28, 1862, and together they had a daughter, Emma Reynolds Moody, and two sons, William Revell Moody and Paul Dwight Moody.

In 1867, the Chicago Y.M.C.A. opened its new three-story Farwell Hall with a 3,500 seat auditorium and large prayer rooms. Moody was a pioneer in allowing women to be involved in

Y.M.C.A. ministry, as well as persons of any race.

Roger F. Dunn wrote in "Formative years of the Chicago Y.M.C.A.: A study in urban history" (1944, *Journal of the Illinois State Historical Society* vol. 37, pp. 349) that their building was "the scene of a constant round of religious meetings, all carried on with revivalistic fervor."

The Y.M.C.A.'s building was a visible beacon in the "cause of temperance, and for the suppression of obscene literature, against 'Sabbath desecration', smoking, theater-going, dancing and billiards." Tragically, it burned down in 1869 and was replaced with a smaller building.

In 1870, Moody encouraged his brother-in-law, Fleming H. Revell, to begin a company to publish his lessons on practical Christian living.

In 1867, Moody made his first trip to Britain, where he met Charles Spurgeon and George Muller.

In June of 1870, at an International Convention of the Y.M.C.A. in Indianapolis, Moody met Gospel singer Ira Sankey. Sankey had been a Union soldier in the Civil War, and was the leader of the Y.M.C.A. in New Castle, Pennsylvania.

When Sankey sang William Cowper's hymn, "There is a fountain filled with blood," Moody was so impressed that he asked Sankey to join him in ministry, singing before his preaching.

Later in 1870, Moody took a second trip to the United Kingdom.

In 1871, the Great Chicago Fire broke out. Tornadoes of fire killed over 300 people and left over 100,000 homeless. Flames engulfed an area four miles wide and a mile across, destroying 17,000 buildings, including the Y.M.C.A.

building and Moody's Illinois Street Church.

Hurricane force winds carried soot, ash, and embers across Lake Michigan, setting fires across the State of Michigan. D.L. Moody said:

> We can stand affliction better than we can prosperity, for in prosperity we forget God.

After the fire, Moody raised money to rebuild the Y.M.C.A., and the church, renaming it the Chicago Avenue Church. It grew in attendance to over 10,000, with 6,000 waiting outside.

Moody and Sankey began traveling the country, holding evangelistic meetings from Chicago to Boston, San Francisco to Vancouver, preaching to hundreds of thousands.

In 1873, Moody made his third trip to Great Britain. While in Dublin he met British revivalist Henry Varley, who told him "The world has yet to see what God can do with a man fully consecrated to him." Moody replied, "By God's help, I aim to be that man."

On January 19, 1876, President Ulysses S. Grant and his cabinet attended Moody's rally. Preaching in New York, the crowds grew so large they needed a bigger building. P.T. Barnum let Moody use his Great Roman Hippodrome, as his circus was not open on Sundays.

When Barnum's Show began traveling, D.L. Moody, with help from banker J.P. Morgan and railroad industrialist Cornelius Vanderbilt, transformed the Great Roman Hippodrome into a revival tabernacle.

Services began February 7, 1876, with 7,000 people in the main hall, 4,000 in overflow, thousands outside, 500 ushers, and 1,200 singers directed by Ira Sankey. Sunday attendance hit 25,000. It was perhaps Moody's most important campaign, for in impacting New York, he impacted the world.

Moody recorded an account:

> I remember when preaching in New York City, at the Hippodrome, a man coming up to me and telling me a story that thrilled my soul.
>
> One night, he said he had been gambling; had gambled all his money away ...
>
> When he went home to the hotel that night he did not sleep much. The next morning happened to be Sunday. He got up, felt bad, couldn't eat anything, didn't touch his breakfast, was miserable, and thought about putting an end to his existence ...
>
> That afternoon he took a walk up Broadway, and when he came to the Hippodrome he saw great crowds going in and thought of entering too ...
>
> When inside he listened to the singing and heard the text, 'Where art thou?' and he thought he would go out. He rose to go, and the text came upon his ears again, 'Where art thou?'
>
> This was too personal, he thought, it was disagreeable, and he made for the door, but as he got to the third row from the entrance, the words came to him again. 'Where art thou?'
>
> He stood still, for the question had come to him with irresistible force, and

God had found him right there. He went to his hotel and prayed all that night, and now he is a bright and shining light.

And this young man, who was a commercial traveler, went back to the village in which he had been reared ... and went around among his friends and acquaintances and testified for Christ, as earnestly and beneficially for him as his conduct had (before) been against Him.

Concerned with the condition of poor minority children, Moody founded Northfield Seminary for Young Ladies in 1879, and Mount Hermon School for Boys in 1881.

In 1886, he sponsored a conference for college students at the Mount Hermon School, sparking the Student Volunteer Movement for Foreign Mission, which, by 1911, sent out 5,000 young people as missionaries around the world.

Chicago White Stocking baseball star Billy Sunday began attending Y.M.C.A. meetings in 1886, which prepared him to be a revival preacher.

In 1872, Moody and Sankey made their first of several trips to England, ministering to tens of thousands. Not being concerned with centuries of religious taboos, they even held meetings in Ireland where there had been a Protestant–Catholic tension for centuries.

While in England, Moody met the missionary to China, Hudson Taylor, and the famous preacher Charles Spurgeon.

In 1892, Moody finished preaching his London revival meetings in Charles Spurgeon's Metropolitan Tabernacle. He and his son, Will, boarded the ocean liner *Spree* and headed for New York. Being fatigued, he questioned within himself if he should preach at the 1893 Chicago World's Fair.

On the third day of the voyage, there was a loud crash and a shock reverberated through the ship. The main shaft had broken and the ship started to sink. Drifting out of the sea lanes, hope of being spotted by passing vessels faded. The ship was taking on so much water the pumps were useless. Lifeboats would capsize in the rough seas.

Passengers gathered on the slanted floor of the main deck and waited for two days. Moody preached faith to the passengers, and shortly after, a ship was spotted coming to their rescue.

After landing back in America, he met with Bible students, saying:

> If you have any regard for me, if you love me, pray for me that God may anoint me for the work in Chicago; I want to be filled with the Spirit that I may preach the Gospel as I never preached it before; we want to see the salvation of God as we have never seen it before.

He later explained:

> As I was preparing to leave London after my last visit there, I called upon a famous physician. He told me that my heart was weakening and that I would have to ease up on my work, that I would have to be more careful of myself; and I was going home with an idea that I would ease up a little.
>
> During the voyage, the announcement

came that our vessel, the *Spree*, was sinking, and we rolled there for two days helplessly.

No one on earth knows what I passed through at the thought that probably my work was finished, and that I would never again have the privilege of preaching the Gospel of Jesus Christ; and on that first dark night after the accident, I made a vow that if God would let me live and bring me back to America, I would go back to Chicago, and at this World's Fair, preach the Gospel with all the power He would give me.

And God has made it possible for me to keep that vow during the past five months. It seems as if I went to the very gates of Heaven during that two days on the sinking ship, and God permitted me to come back and preach His Son a little longer.

Moody's preaching at the 1893 Chicago World's Fair was the capstone of his ministry. He wrote:

We have today everything to encourage us, and nothing to discourage us. This has been by far the best week we have had. The Gospel has, through this agency, been brought to 150,000 people during the week.

I have never seen greater eagerness to hear the word of God. The largest halls are too small for the crowds that come to many of the services.

One night, for instance, on my way to the Fair Grounds, I beheld one of the most beautiful sights I have ever seen on earth. It was a wonderful display of fireworks and illuminations, tens of thousands of people gazing on the scene.

It seemed useless to expect any one to come away from that scene and sit down in a tabernacle to hear the Gospel; but the house was filled, and we had a blessed meeting ...

The following nights though cold and rainy, with a damp, uncomfortable room, the people crowded in until every inch of space was occupied.

I thank God that I am living in Chicago today; these have been the happiest moments of my life; what a work He has given us today; what encouragements He has given us; how He has blessed us.

Perhaps never in your life will some of you have an opportunity to do as much for Christ as now.

In 1893, a new 13 story Y.M.C.A. building was constructed. It had boarding rooms for 400 members to stay there, a Grand Hall seating 1,500, a gymnasium, a bowling alley, baths, parlors, canteens, restaurants, a library with 20,000 books, teaching and lecture rooms, an art gallery, artist studios, an apartment for the General Secretary, and a flat for the janitor's family.

D.L. Moody died December 22, 1899. During his lifetime, through preaching, literature and schools he founded, Moody reached an estimated 100 million. Some of his memorable quotes are:

> "A ship lives in the water; but if the water gets into the ship, she goes to the bottom. So Christians may live in the world, but if the world gets into them, they sink."

"There are many of us that are willing to do great things for the Lord, but few of us are willing to do little things."

"God doesn't seek for golden vessels ... but He must have clean ones."

"The Bible will keep you from sin, or sin will keep you from the Bible."

"Treat the Lord Jesus Christ as a personal friend. His is not a creed, a mere doctrine, but it is He Himself we have."

"Preparation for old age should begin no later than one's teens. A life which is empty of purpose until 65 will not suddenly become filled on retirement."

"I know the Bible is inspired because it inspires me."

"Faith makes all things possible ... Love makes all things easy."

"It is the greatest pleasure of living to win souls to Christ."

"God never made a promise that was too good to be true."

"The law tells me how crooked I am. Grace comes along and straightens me out."

"The sun is light, and can't help shining; God is Love, and He can't help loving."

"Death may be the King of terrors ... but Jesus is the King of kings!"

"The monument I want after I am dead is a monument with two legs going around the world—a saved sinner telling about the salvation of Jesus Christ."

Dwight Moody wrote in *Secret Power: or the Secret of Success in Christian Life and Work* (Chicago: Fleming H. Revell, 1881):

> We read that the fruit of the Spirit is love. God is love, Christ is love ... What a blessed attribute is this.
>
> May I call it the dome of the temple of the graces. Better still, it is the crown of crowns worn by the Triune God.
>
> Human love is a natural emotion which flows forth towards the object of our affections. But Divine love is as high above human love as the heaven is above the earth.
>
> The natural man is of the earth, earthly, and however pure his love may be, it is weak and imperfect at best.
>
> But the love of God is perfect and entire, wanting nothing. It is as a mighty ocean in its greatness, dwelling with and flowing from the Eternal Spirit.

James Findlay, author of *Dwight L. Moody, American Evangelist, 1837–1899* (1969) wrote:

> For Moody the third person of the Trinity manifested himself in the world chiefly as the love of God shining in and through individual Christian lives. As he once put it: "You can sum up

all the fruits of the Spirit in one word — Love."

The Chicago Bible Institute founded by Moody was renamed after his death to the Moody Bible Institute, with R.A. Torrey as its president.

Chicago Avenue Church was renamed The Moody Church in 1906. It continues to have an international impact with notable leaders such as pastor emeritus Dr. Erwin W. Lutzer, who stated:

> There is more grace in God's heart than there is sin in your past. You become stronger only when you become weaker. When you surrender your will to God, you discover the resources to do what God requires.

Moody, who supported Jewish resettlement of their homeland, stated:

> Moses spent 40 years thinking he was somebody; 40 years learning he was nobody; and 40 years discovering what God can do with a nobody.

Y.M.C.A. DURING THE SPANISH–AMERICAN WAR

Slavery ended in America with the Civil War, but it continued in Cuba. President Ulysses S. Grant stated December 2, 1872:

> Slavery in Cuba is ... a terrible evil ... It is greatly to be hoped that ... Spain

> will voluntarily adopt ... emancipation ... in sympathy with the other powers of the Christian and civilized world.

Grant said December 1, 1873:

> Several thousand persons illegally held as slaves in Cuba ... The slaveholders of Havana ... are vainly striving to stay the march of ideas which has terminated slavery in Christendom, Cuba only excepted.

In 1878, the Spanish Government crushed the revolt, ending "The Ten Years War" in which over 200,000 died. Another "Little War" took place in 1879. Under international pressure, Spain ended slavery by Royal decree in 1886.

In 1895, open rebellion against Spain broke out in Cuba. Spain sent Governor Valeriano Weyler to smash freedom-loving Cubans. Weyler rounded up nearly 300,000 Cubans and forced them into crowded concentration camps.

Between 1896–1897, nearly a third of Cuba's population was in concentration camps, with an estimated 225,000 dying of starvation, exposure, dysentery, and diseases like yellow fever. Pleas for help reached the United States.

President McKinley responded by sending the *USS Maine* to Havana's harbor, which blew up under suspicious conditions, February 15, 1898. He issued the Resolution, April 20, 1898:

> Whereas the abhorrent conditions which have existed for more than three years in the island of Cuba, so near our own borders, have shocked the moral sense of the people of the United States, have been a disgrace to Christian civilization, culminating, as

they have, in the destruction of a United States battle ship, with 266 of its officers and crew, while on a friendly visit in the harbor of Havana, and cannot longer be endured ...

Resolved ... that the people of the island of Cuba are and of right ought to be free.

Assistant Secretary of Navy Theodore Roosevelt resigned and organized the first volunteer cavalry, the Rough Riders, made up of polo riders, cowboys, blacks, and Indians. It was among the regiments that charged and captured Cuba's Kettle Hill and San Juan Hill, July 1, 1898.

The Gatling Gun was used for the first time. Fighting went on for eight hours. Afterwards there were 1,500 American casualties. Lt. John J. "Black Jack" Pershing, who later rose to the highest rank of General of the Armies, described:

> The entire command moved forward as coolly as though the buzzing of bullets was the humming of bees ...
>
> ... white regiments, black regiments, regulars and Rough Riders, representing the young manhood of the North and the South, fought shoulder to shoulder, unmindful of race or color, unmindful of whether commanded by ex-Confederate or not, and mindful of only their common duty as Americans.

Among the thousands of Americans who volunteered during the Spanish American War were 5,000 black soldiers called "Buffalo Soldiers," a name given to them by the Indians.

The Armed Services Y.M.C.A. website

(asymca.org/about/history, accessed 1/14/25) details the history:

> In the spring of 1898, the Y.M.C.A. mobilized in support of the Spanish–American war in cooperation with military leaders, with more than 500 Y.M.C.A. workers sent overseas.
>
> The Y.M.C.A. moved so quickly that their supplies arrived in Cuba and the Philippines before many of the Army's own supplies.
>
> The work for soldiers and sailors during the Spanish–American War was so highly regarded that the Y.M.C.A.'s central body, following the close of the war in late 1898, established a permanent Army and Navy Committee to give national direction to the work, which resulted in rapidly expanding peacetime development.
>
> During the Spanish–American War, the American Red Cross cared for the survivors of the *USS Maine* explosion, established orphanages, and provided medical supplies, food, and aid to military and civilians.
>
> The Salvation Army also served during the Spanish–American War, accompanying troops to the Philippines.

In recognition of the Y.M.C.A. contributions, in 1902, Congress authorized Y.M.C.A. buildings to be constructed on military installations, with thirty-one Army and Navy Y.M.C.A. chapters serving soldiers and sailors across the nation.

RED CROSS DURING THE SPANISH-AMERICAN WAR

During the Spanish–American War, 1898, Clara Barton and The American Red Cross helped in hospitals in Cuba. She wrote:

> An institution or reform movement that is not selfish, must originate in the recognition of some evil that is adding to the sum of human suffering, or diminishing the sum of happiness.

She explained:

> In time of peace we must prepare for war, and it is no less a wise benevolence that makes preparation in the hour of peace for assuaging the ills that are sure to accompany war.

President William McKinley mentioned Clara Barton in his Annual Message, December 5, 1898:

> It is a pleasure for me to mention in terms of cordial appreciation the timely and useful work of the American National Red Cross, both in relief measures preparatory to the campaigns, in sanitary assistance at several of the camps of assemblage, and later, under the able and experienced leadership of the president of the society, Miss Clara Barton, on the fields of battle and in the hospitals at the front in Cuba ...
>
> Working in conjunction with the governmental authorities ... and with the enthusiastic cooperation of many

patriotic women and societies in the various States, the Red Cross has fully maintained its already high reputation for intense earnestness and ability to exercise the noble purposes of its international organization,

thus justifying the confidence and support which it has received at the hands of the American people ...

McKinley continued:

To the members and officers of this society and all who aided them in their philanthropic work the sincere and lasting gratitude of the soldiers and the public is due and is freely accorded.

In tracing these events we are constantly reminded of our obligations to the Divine Master for His watchful care over us and His safe guidance, for which the nation makes reverent acknowledgment and offers humble prayer for the continuance of His favor.

THEODORE ROOSEVELT & MORAL STRENGTH

No one embodied Muscular Christianity more than President Theodore Roosevelt, who was born October 27, 1858. His father, Theodore Roosevelt, Sr., was a successful New York businessman who helped raise support for the Union during the Civil War. He taught an evangelistic class called

Mission Sabbath School.

Young Theodore was baptized April 21, 1860, in New York's Madison Square Presbyterian Church, described in Miriam Berman's *Madison Square: The Park and Its Celebrated Landmarks* as "one of the wealthiest congregations in the country." All four Roosevelt children were faithful in Sunday school attendance there, as cited in Roosevelt's *Autobiography,*

As a child, Theodore had debilitating asthma, waking up at night feeling he was being smothered to death. At 6-years-old, he looked out the window of his grandfather's mansion in Union Square, New York City, to see Abraham Lincoln's funeral procession.

Home-schooled as a child, Theodore saw a dead seal in the market and became fascinated with animals and zoology.

In 1873, his family attended the Collegiate Dutch Reformed Church of St. Nicholas in New York City, as well as the Fifth Avenue Presbyterian Church. His family spent summers in Oyster Bay, New York. In 1874, they began attending First Presbyterian Church of Oyster Bay.

Theodore considered his father like the character "Greatheart" in John Bunyan's novel *The Pilgrim's Progress,* describing him in his diary, January 2, 1878, as "the best, wisest and most loving of men, the type of all that is noble, brave, wise, and good." Theodore added:

> My father, Theodore Roosevelt, was the best man I ever knew. He combined strength and courage with gentleness, tenderness, and great

unselfishness. He would not tolerate in us children selfishness or cruelty, idleness, cowardice, or untruthfulness.

His father took the family on trips to Europe in 1869 and 1870, and Egypt in 1872. Theodore, at the age of 15, wrote of their trip to Jerusalem:

> In the afternoon we went to the Wailing Place of the Jews.

His father helped found the New York Orthopedic Hospital, the Museum of Natural History, and supported the Children's Aid Society. He funded the Newsboys' Lodging House, which cared for hundreds of stray boys who scraped a living by shining shoes and selling newspapers, as mentioned in Horatio Alger's famous novel *Ragged Dick; or, Street Life in New York with the Boot Blacks,* 1868.

At age 16, Theodore became a member of the church where his father had him baptized as a child. At this time, he was accosted by older boys while on a camping trip. His father encouraged him to begin exercising, and he became a skilled boxer and a third-degree brown belt in judo.

In 1876, he entered Harvard. While there, he taught a weekly Sunday school class for four years at Christ Church in Cambridge, Massachusetts.

In 1878, he was devastated to receive the news of his father's sudden death. He cherished his father's lasting advice:

> Take care of your morals first, your health next, and finally your studies.

After graduation, Theodore Roosevelt attended Columbia University Law School in

New York. At the age of 20, he attended Fifth Avenue Presbyterian Church, admiring the sermons of Dr. John Hall. He commented,

> I like our simple Presbyterian form for the service so much, for it always makes me think.

In 1882, at the age of 23, he wrote a significant book, *The Naval War of 1812.* The book was so well received that just four years later, the U.S. Navy ordered a copy to be placed on every ship.

It influenced Rear Admiral Alfred Thayer Mahan to write *The Influence of Sea Power Upon the French Revolution and Empire, 1793–1812* (published in 1892), which revolutionized naval warfare by causing the United States, Britain and Germany to upgrade their navies.

Roosevelt became interested in politics, and began attending meetings of New York's 21st District Republican Association.

When 20th President, Republican James Garfield, was assassinated in 1881 and Vice-President Chester Arthur assumed the Presidency, Roosevelt decided to run for state assemblyman.

When he won in 1882, he decided to drop out of law school to pursue politics. He was reelected in 1883, and in 1884, the year Democrat Grover Cleveland was elected the 22nd U.S. President.

In 1880, Theodore married Alice Hathaway Lee. Four years later, in 1884, their daughter, Alice Lee Roosevelt, was born. Tragically, two days after her birth, on February 14, 1884, Roosevelt's mother, Mittie, died of typhoid in the morning, and that afternoon, in the same house, his wife, Alice, died of kidney failure.

Roosevelt scratched in his diary a large black "X" with the words "The light has gone out of my life." Two thousand people attended the joint funeral of Theodore's wife and mother at New York's Fifth Avenue Presbyterian Church.

Roosevelt attended the Republican National Convention in June of 1884. He gave a speech in support of John Roy Lynch, an African–American former slave, recommending that he be chosen as the temporary chair of the Convention.

After bitter political battles, Roosevelt retired from politics, left his baby daughter with his sister, and went to ranch in the Dakotas.

Roosevelt described the muscular life of cowboys in *Ranch Life and the Hunting Trail,* 1888:

> The whole existence is patriarchal in character: it is the life of men who live in the open, who tend their herds on horseback, who go armed and ready to guard their lives by their own prowess, whose wants are very simple, and who call no man master.
>
> Ranching is an occupation like those of vigorous, primitive pastoral peoples, having little in common with the humdrum, workaday business world of the nineteenth century ...
>
> The moral tone of a cow-camp, indeed, is rather high than otherwise. Meanness, cowardice, and dishonesty are not tolerated.
>
> There is a high regard for truthfulness and keeping one's word, intense contempt for any kind of hypocrisy, and a hearty

dislike for a man who shirks his work.

Many of the men gamble and drink, but many do neither; and the conversation is not worse than in most bodies composed wholly of male human beings.

A cowboy will not submit tamely to an insult, and is ever ready to avenge his own wrongs; nor has he an overwrought fear of shedding blood.

He possesses, in fact, few of the emasculated, milk-and-water moralities admired by the pseudo-philanthropists; but he does possess, to a very high degree, the stern, manly qualities that are invaluable to a nation.

While there, he also wrote: *Hunting Trips of a Ranchman,* 1885, and *The Wilderness Hunter,* 1891. He bought a herd and ranched for three years, till the severe winter of 1886–1887 killed most of his cattle.

He returned east and married childhood friend Edith Kermit Carow on December 2, 1886, at St George's Church in Hanover Square, London.

Together they had five children, and also raised daughter Alice from his first marriage.

When at home in Sagamore Hill, he attended his wife's church, Christ Episcopal Church in Oyster Bay. Edith mentioned she was impressed with Theodore's "deep knowledge of the Bible."

In 1886, he ran for Mayor of New York City, but lost. He wrote another book *The Winning of the West,* 1889.

Roosevelt campaigned for Republican Benjamin Harrison, who won to be the 23rd U.S. President. Harrison appointed Roosevelt to the

United States Civil Service Commission.

In 1892, Grover Cleveland won his second term as the 24th President. Though a Democrat, Cleveland reappointed Roosevelt, a Republican, to the same position.

Before organized crime, such as the mafia, came to New York, the local police "ran" the crime in their districts.

In 1894, the New York Mayor appointed Roosevelt to the City Police Commissioners, where he became president of the board, insisting on law and order. He reformed the department, cleaned out corruption, and installed telephones in station houses. He walked officers' beats on the streets after midnight to make sure they were on duty. On Sundays, he made sure all stores were closed to comply with New York's Blue Laws promoting observance of the Lord's day of worship.

Roosevelt was the first to bring Jews into the police force, calling them his "Maccabees."

Journalist Jacob Riis of the *Evening Sun* newspaper, wrote in his book *How the Other Half Lives*, of the terrible conditions the millions of immigrants suffered:

> When Roosevelt read my book, he came ... No one ever helped as he did. For two years we were brothers in (New York City's crime-ridden) Mulberry Street ...
>
> There is very little ease where Theodore Roosevelt leads, as we all found out.
>
> The lawbreaker found it out ... and lived to respect him ... For the first time a moral purpose came into the street. In the light of it everything was transformed.

In 1897, when William McKinley became the 25th President, he appointed Roosevelt as the Assistant Secretary of the Navy. With the help of Alfred Thayer Mahan, Roosevelt built up the U.S. Navy, especially battleships.

On February 15, 1898, *USS Maine* exploded in Cuba's Havana Harbor, beginning the Spanish–American War.

Roosevelt immediately sent orders for the Navy to prepare for war. Admiral George Dewey later credited this as a key factor in quick victory in the Battle of Manila Bay. He then resigned as Assistant Secretary of the Navy and organized the first Volunteer Cavalry, "the Rough Riders," which helped capture Cuba's San Juan Hill.

Upon his return to New York in 1898, Roosevelt ran for Governor and won. In the 1900 Republican Convention, he was chosen to be the Vice-Presidential running-mate for William McKinley's reelection.

When McKinley was assassinated on September 6, 1901, Roosevelt became America's youngest President. As the 26th U.S. President, Roosevelt, a Republican, invited the first black man to be an honored guest to dine in the White House on October 16, 1901, Booker T. Washington.

Southern Democrat newspapers condemned Roosevelt, as printed in *The Memphis Scimitar*:

> The most damnable outrage which has ever been perpetrated by any citizen of the United States was committed yesterday by the President, when he invited a n– to dine with him at the White House.

> It would not be worth more than a passing notice if Theodore Roosevelt had sat down to dinner in his own home with a Pullman car porter, but Roosevelt the individual and Roosevelt the President are not to be viewed in the same light.

Booker T. Washington wrote to President Roosevelt, October 26, 1901:

> I have refrained from writing you regarding the now famous dinner in which both of us ate so innocently ... I believe that a great deal is being made over the incident because of the elections which are now pending in several Southern states.

Roosevelt responded to the criticism:

> The only wise and honorable and Christian thing to do is to treat each black man and each white man strictly on his merits as a man.

Roosevelt addressed the Long Island Bible Society in 1901, explaining that the Bible was not only "essential to Christianity but essential to good citizenship." He continued:

> Every thinking man ... realizes ... that the teachings of the Bible are so interwoven and entwined with our whole civic and social life that it would be literally — I do not mean figuratively, I mean literally — impossible for us to figure to ourselves what that life would be if these teachings were removed.
>
> We would lose almost all the standards

by which we now judge both public and private morals; all the standards toward which we, with more or less of resolution, strive to raise ourselves.

Almost every man who has by his lifework added to the sum of human achievement of which the race is proud, has based his lifework largely upon the teachings of the Bible ...

Among the greatest men a disproportionately large number have been diligent and close students of the Bible at first hand.

Roosevelt took on his era's version of globalist elites by being a "trust-buster," breaking up monopolies, such as John D. Rockefeller's Standard Oil Company. He settleed labor disputes and exposed deep-state corruption in the Bureau of Indian Affairs, Land Office, and Post Office.

After Upton Sinclair's book *The Jungle*, 1906, Roosevelt harnessed public opinion to pass the Meat Inspection Act and Pure Food and Drug Act.

On March 17, 1905, St. Patrick's Day, Theodore Roosevelt gave away in marriage his deceased brother's daughter, Eleanor, to wed her fifth cousin, once removed, Franklin D. Roosevelt.

Capitalizing on Theodore's name, Franklin rose in politics to become the 32nd U.S. President.

Theodore Roosevelt is considered the first "conservationist president." He created the U.S. Forest Service, designating: 5 National Parks; 18 U.S. National Monuments; 51 bird reserves, 4 game preserves, 150 National Forests, being responsible for 121 forest reserves in 31 states.

He placed 230,000,000 acres under public protection and established 150 million acres of reserved forestry land.

In his foreign policy, he assisted in 1904 to negotiate a Japan–Russian Treaty, for which he won the Nobel Peace Prize.

He intervened in the First Moroccan Crisis, the Venezuelan Crisis, and settled disputes with Britain over the Alaskan border. He helped Panama separate from Columbia, and began building the Panama Canal.

Roosevelt argued for the protection of Jews of North Africa. Ambassador Michael B. Oren noted in *Power, Faith and Fantasy*, that in Roosevelt's negotiations with Morocco, he insisted they:

> ... secured his country's customary concerns in the area, protecting North African Jews from oppression and American merchants from unfair restrictions and fees.

He pressured Romania and Russia to treat their Jewish populations fairly. After a massacre of Jews in Kishinev, in the Bessarabia Governorate of the Russian Empire, Roosevelt wrote:

> I need not dwell upon a fact so patent as the widespread indignation with which the Americans heard of the dreadful outrages up on the Jews in Kishineff.

In 1906, Roosevelt became the first president to appoint a Jew to his Cabinet, Secretary of Commerce and Labor Oscar Solomon Straus, who with his brother owned Macy's Department Store.

He wrote to Straus:

I don't know whether you know it or not, but I want you to become a member of my Cabinet. I have a very high estimate of your character, your judgment and your ability, and I want you for personal reasons. There is still a further reason: I want to show Russia and some other countries what we think of Jews in this country.

Roosevelt stated:

> To discriminate against a thoroughly upright citizen because he belongs to some particular Church, or because, like Abraham Lincoln, he has not avowed his allegiance to any Church, is an outrage against the liberty of conscience ...
>
> In my Cabinet at the present moment there sit side by side Catholic and Protestant, Christian and Jew, each man chosen because in my belief he is peculiarly fit to exercise on behalf of all our people the duties of the office.

In 1910, a proposal was made to add a religious designation to passports. It was opposed by American Jews, who were denied entrance into Russia. Roosevelt opposed this, writing to Israel Fischer, June 30, 1911:

> I would not put in the word Hebrew. I believe that from the standpoint of the Christian, just as much as from the standpoint of the Jew, it is ill-advised to treat what is really a religious matter as a race matter.
>
> I know plenty of men, some of them very prominent men, who are of mixed

race; and personally I should no more have a man entered on a passport as a Hebrew, than as an Episcopalian, or a Baptist, or a Roman Catholic.

Roosevelt wrote:

> It seems to me that it is entirely proper to start a Zionist State around Jerusalem.

In "Nine Reasons Why Men Should Go To Church" for *The Ladies' Home Journal*, he wrote:

> Church work and Church attendance mean the cultivation of the habit of feeling some responsibility for others and the sense of braced moral strength, which prevents a relaxation of one's own moral fiber.

As a member of Grace Dutch Reformed Church in D.C., Roosevelt stated in 1909:

> After a week on perplexing problems ... it does so rest my soul to come into the house of The Lord and to sing and mean it, "Holy, Holy, Holy, Lord God Almighty" ...
>
> (My) great joy and glory that, in occupying an exalted position in the nation, I am enabled, to preach the practical moralities of the Bible to my fellow-countrymen and to hold up Christ as the hope and Savior of the world.

Roosevelt told the Centennial Meeting of the Board of Home Missions of the Presbyterian Church at Carnegie Hall, New York, May 20, 1902:

> Every earnest and zealous believer, every man or woman who is a doer of

the work and not a hearer only, is a lifelong missionary in his or her field of labor ... (They) are doing strong men's work as they bring the light of civilization into the world's dark places.

G.K. Chesterton wrote in the *Illustrated London News*, January 14, 1911:

The true soldier fights not because he hates what is in front of him, but because he loves what is behind him.

Theodore Roosevelt, laying the cornerstone of the House of Representatives office building, April 14, 1906, addressed the human tendency to wallow in self-pity and obsess over misfortune rather than moving forward in faith.

In Bunyan's *Pilgrim's Progress* you may recall the description of the man with the muck-rake, the man who could look no way but downward, with the muck-rake in his hand, who was offered a celestial crown for his muck-rake, but who would neither look up nor regard the crown he was offered, but continued to rake to himself the filth of the floor.

On December 6, 1904, Roosevelt told Congress:

No Christian and civilized community can afford to show a happy-go-lucky lack of concern for the youth of today; for, if so, the community will have to pay a terrible penalty of financial burden and social degradation in the tomorrow.

Roosevelt championed muscular Christianity

in his book *The Foes of Our Own Household,* 1917, which included his address to the Holy Name Society, August 16, 1903:

> I am not addressing weaklings, or I should not take the trouble to come here. I am addressing strong, vigorous men, who are engaged in the active hard work of life ... men who ... have strength to set a right example to others ...
>
> You cannot retain your self-respect if you are loose and foul of tongue, that a man who is to lead a clean and honorable life must inevitably suffer if his speech likewise is not clean and honorable ...
>
> A man must be clean of mouth as well as clean of life — must show by his words as well as by his actions his fealty (loyalty) to the Almighty ...
>
> We have good Scriptural authority for the statement that it is not what comes into a man's mouth but what goes out of it that counts ...

He added:

> Every man here knows the temptations that beset all of us in this world. At times any man will slip.
>
> I do not expect perfection, but I do expect genuine and sincere effort toward being decent and cleanly in thought, in word, and in deed ... I expect you to be strong. I would not respect you if you were not.
>
> I do not want to see Christianity professed only by weaklings; I want

> to see it a moving spirit among men of strength ...

Roosevelt continued:

> I should hope to see each man ... become all the fitter to do the rough work of the world ... and if, which may Heaven forfend, war should come, all the fitter to fight ... I desire to see in this country the decent men strong, and the strong men decent ...
>
> There is always a tendency among very young men ... to think that to be wicked is rather smart; to think it shows that they are men ...
>
> Oh, how often you see some young fellow who boasts that he is going to "see life," meaning by that that he is going to see that part of life which it is a thousandfold better should remain unseen!
>
> I ask that every man here constitute himself his brother's keeper by setting an example to that younger brother which will prevent him from getting such a false estimate of life. Example is the most potent of all things.
>
> If any one of you are in the presence of younger boys, and ... misbehave yourself, if you use coarse and blasphemous language before them, you can be sure that these younger people will follow your example and not your precept.
>
> It is no use to preach to them if you do not act decently yourself ... The most effective way in which you can preach is by your practice ...

> The father, the elder brothers, the friends, can do much toward seeing that the boys as they become men become clean and honorable men ...

Roosevelt concluded:

> I have told you that I wanted you not only to be decent, but to be strong. These boys will not admire virtue of a merely anemic type. They believe in courage, in manliness.
>
> They admire those who have the quality of being brave, the quality of facing life as life should be faced, the quality that must stand at the root of good citizenship in peace or in war.
>
> If you are to be effective as good Christians you must possess strength and courage, or your example will count for little with the young ... I want to see every man able to hold his own with the strong, and also ashamed to oppress the weak ...
>
> I want to see him too strong of spirit to submit to wrong ... I want to see each man able to hold his own in the rough work of actual life outside, and also, when he is at home, a good man, unselfish in dealing with wife, or mother, or children.
>
> Remember that the preaching does not count if it is not backed up by practice. There is no good in your preaching to your boys to be brave, if you run away.

After his Presidency, he helped William Howard Taft to be elected the 27th President.

Roosevelt then led a Smithsonian safari in Africa in 1909. He then traveled to meet world leaders, from Egypt to Austrian–Hungarian Emperor Franz Joseph, Germany's Kaiser Wilhelm II, England's King George V.

In St. Louis, Missouri, 1910, Roosevelt was the first person who had been President to fly in an airplane. He ran for President again in 1912 on the Bull Moose Party ticket, with his platform being:

> To destroy this invisible Government,
> to dissolve the unholy alliance between
> corrupt business and corrupt politics.

At a campaign speech in Milwaukee, October 14, 1912, a saloonkeeper shot Roosevelt in the chest. He survived, as the bullet did not hit any vital organs. In his blood-stained shirt, Roosevelt stood back up and finished his speech.

The Bull Moose Party unfortunately split the Republican Party, allowing Democrat Woodrow Wilson to be elected the 28th President.

Europe was heading toward World War. Winston Churchill transitioned the British Navy from coal to oil. Since oil was just discovered in Iran, Churchill arranged in 1908 the Anglo–Iranian Oil Company, or British Petroleum.

Kaiser Wilhelm II industrialized Germany and also needed oil. He made a treaty with the Ottoman Turkish Sultan Abdul Hamid the Second to build a Berlin–Baghdad Railway

On June 28, 1914, Austria's Archduke Franz Ferdinand was assassinated in Sarajevo, beginning World War I. Half of the War took place in the Middle East. In the Ottoman Empire, three

"Young Turk" Pashas orchestrated the massacre of millions of Kurds, Assyrians, Syrians, and Armenians.

Roosevelt wrote:

> "... peace could only be real when the Armenians and the Arabs were given their independence, and the Jews given control of Palestine."

Theodore Roosevelt wrote in *Fear God and Take Your Own Part* (NY: G.H. Doran Co., 1916):

> Armenians ... for some centuries have sedulously (persistently) avoided militarism and war ... are so suffering precisely and exactly because they have been pacifists whereas their neighbors, the Turks, have not been pacifists but militarists.

Roosevelt criticized Woodrow Wilson's Administration for abandoning Armenia:

> Armenians, have been subjected to wrongs far greater than any that have been committed since the close of the Napoleonic Wars ... the wars of Genghis Khan and Tamerlane in Asia. Yet this government has not raised its hand to do anything to help the people who were wronged ...
>
> This course of national infamy ... began when the last Administration surrendered to the peace at-any-price people, and started the negotiation of its foolish and wicked all inclusive arbitration treaties ...
>
> Individuals and nations who preach the doctrine of milk-and-water invariably have in them a softness of fiber which means that

they fear to antagonize those who preach and practice the doctrine of blood-and-iron." (T. Roosevelt, *Fear God*, p. 111)

Theodore Roosevelt wrote in *Fear God and Take Your Part*, 1916:

> Christianity is not the creed of Asia and Africa at this moment solely because the seventh century Christians of Asia and Africa had trained themselves not to fight, whereas the Muslims were trained to fight.
>
> Christianity was saved in Europe solely because the peoples of Europe fought.
>
> If the peoples of Europe in the 7th and 8th centuries, and on up to and including the 17th century, had not possessed a military equality with, and gradually a growing superiority over the Mohammedans who invaded Europe, Europe would at this moment be Mohammedan and the Christian religion would be exterminated.

He added:

> Wherever the Mohammedans have had complete sway, wherever the Christians have been unable to resist them by the sword, Christianity has ultimately disappeared ...
>
> From the hammer of Charles Martel to the sword of Jan Sobieski, Christianity owed its safety in Europe to the fact that it was able to show that it could and would fight as well as the Mohammedan aggressor.

As America was preparing to enter World War I, the New York Bible Society published a pocket *New Testament and Book of Psalms* in 1917 to be handed out to all the U.S. soldiers, with Theodore

Roosevelt writing the introduction:

> The teachings of the New Testament are foreshadowed in Micah's verse (Micah 6:8): "What more does the Lord require of thee than to do justice, and to love mercy, and to walk humbly with thy God?"
>
> DO JUSTICE; and therefore fight valiantly against the armies of Germany and Turkey, for these nations in this crisis stand for the reign of Moloch and Beelzebub on this earth.
>
> LOVE MERCY; treat prisoners well, succor the wounded, treat every woman as if she was your sister, care for the little children, and be tender to the old and helpless.
>
> WALK HUMBLY; You will do so if you study the life and teachings of the Savior. May the God of justice and mercy have you in His keeping.

Roosevelt's son Quentin was a pilot in Europe during the War, but was tragically shot down, July 14, 1918. Theodore Roosevelt died less than six months later, on January 6, 1919, at the age of 60.

His son Archie Roosevelt telegrammed his older brother Kermit Roosevelt "The old lion is dead." Vice-President Thomas R. Marshall stated:

> Death had to take Roosevelt sleeping, for if he had been awake, there would have been a fight.

Franklin Roosevelt wrote January 19, 1936:

> When Theodore Roosevelt died, the Secretary of his class at Harvard, in sending classmates a notice of his passing, added

this quotation from Pilgrim's Progress:

> "My sword I give to him that shall succeed me in my pilgrimage, and my courage and skill to him that can get it. My marks and scars I carry with me, to be a witness for me that I have fought His battles who now will be my rewarder."

Theodore Roosevelt once wrote that it was:

> ... not the critic who counts ... who points out ... where the doer of deeds could have done them better ... (but) the man in the arena whose face is marred by dust and sweat ... who errs and comes short ... but who does actually strive to do the deeds.

In 1909, Roosevelt stated:

> The thought of modern industry in the hands of Christian charity is a dream worth dreaming. The thought of industry in the hands of paganism is a nightmare beyond imagining. The choice between the two is upon us.

RUDYARD KIPLING'S CAPTAIN COURAGEOUS

Rudyard Kipling was born in British India in 1865. His grandparents on both sides were Methodist ministers. At the age of five, his parents sent him back to England to be raised in a boarding school.

Poor eyesight ended young Kipling's hopes

of a British military career, so in 1882, at the age of 16, he returned to India as a journalist. He wrote for *The Civil and Military Gazette* in Lahore, and in 1886, published his first collection Departmental Ditties.

At the age of 22, he published numerous collections of stories: *Plain Tales from the Hills; Soldiers Three; The Story of the Gadsbys; In Black and White; Under the Deodars; The Phantom Rickshaw;* and *Wee Willie Winkie.*

In 1889, Kipling left India and traveled to Rangoon, Singapore, Hong Kong, and Japan, finally landing in San Francisco. From there, he traveled across the United States to New York, where he met Mark Twain. He fell in love with his friend's sister, Caroline Balestier.

Rudyard and Caroline married in 1892 and settled in Vermont, where two of their children were born. He wrote captivating stories, such as: *The Jungle Book*, 1894; *The Second Jungle Book*, 1895; *The Man Who Would Be King*, 1888; *Kim*, 1901; *Gunga Din*, 1890; *Mandalay*, 1890.

In 1896, Kipling moved his family back to England. Once a year they would go on a winter holiday to South Africa. There, Kipling gained first hand knowledge of the Boer War, in which Sir Baden-Powell fought.

Kipling declined King George the Fifth's offer of knighthood, Poet Laureate and Order of Merit. In 1907, at the age of 41, he was the youngest recipient of the Nobel Prize for Literature.

His 6-year-old daughter Josephine died of pneumonia. His 18-year-old son, John, was killed in the World War I Battle of Loos, October 8, 1915.

Kipling encouraged American soldiers at a Y.M.C.A. officers hut, with *The New York Times* publishing the article, December 29, 1918, "KIPLING PRAISES WORK OF Y.M.C.A."

He published *Captains Courageous: A Story of the Grand Banks* in 1897. Theodore Roosevelt, in his essay "What We Can Expect of the American Boy" (May, 1900), praised Kipling for describing "in the liveliest way just what a boy should be and do."

The story begins with the spoiled 15-year-old Harvey Cheyne, Jr., the son of a California railroad tycoon, who is washed overboard from a transatlantic steamship into the North Atlantic.

He was saved from drowning by a Portuguese fishing schooner named *We're Here*, off the Grand Banks of Newfoundland,

Harvey told them he was wealthy and tried to get them to immediately take him to port.

The captain, Disko Troop, did not believe him and refused. Harvey made matters worse by accusing the captain of taking his money, though he actually left it on the deck of the steamship that he had been washed from.

Captain Troop punches the young brat in the nose, and puts him to work with the crew till they get to port. Harvey eventually comes to grips with his fate. Kipling wrote:

> Like many other unfortunate young people, Harvey had never in all his life received a direct order—never, at least, without long, and sometimes tearful, explanations of the advantages of obedience and the reasons for the request.

Adventures and trials followed, with the captain's son, Dan Troop, helping Harvey get acclimated to the fisherman's life.

> Men who are accustomed to eat at tiny tables in howling gales ... They cleaned up the plates and pans ... sliced pork for the midday meal, swabbed down the foresail, filled the lamps, drew coal and water for the cook, and investigated the fore-hold, where the boat's stores were stacked.
>
> It was another perfect day ... and Harvey breathed to the very bottom of his lungs.

Harvey is a quick learner, becomes skillful, and helps with the ship's accounting of its catch.

> "Where are the fish, though?"
> "'In the sea they say, in the boats we pray,' said Dan, quoting a fisherman's proverb."

Kipling weaves in stories of New England whaling and cod fishing:

> "On a calm sea, every man is a pilot."

> "The trouble with our times is that the future is not what it used to be."

When the ship, *We're Here* finally returns to port, young Harvey wires his parents. They rush to Boston, then to the fishing village of Gloucester, only to be amazed at their son's maturity.

Kipling wrote:

> Real freedom lies in wildness, not in civilization.

The father rewards the seaman who rescued Harvey. The novel ends with the father hiring the captain's son, Dan Troop, to work on his impressive tea clipper fleet and young Harvey goes off to Stanford College in preparation to take over his father's shipping lines.

Theodore Roosevelt wrote in an essay "What We Can Expect of the American Boy" (*Archive of American Journalism Collection*, May, 1900):

> Kipling's ... "Captains Courageous," describes in the liveliest way just what a boy should be and do.
>
> The hero is painted in the beginning as the spoiled, over-indulged child of wealthy parents, of a type which we do sometimes unfortunately see, and than which there exist few things more objectionable on the face of the broad earth.
>
> This boy is afterward thrown on his own resources, amid wholesome surroundings, and is forced to work hard among boys and men who are real boys and real men doing real work. The effect is invaluable.

Ronald Reagan, upon ending his term as President, gave a speech, December 13, 1988:

> As I prepare to lay down the mantle of office ... I cannot help believe that what Rudyard Kipling said of another time and place is true today for America:
>
> "We are at the opening verse of the opening page of the chapter of endless possibilities."

HORATIO ALGER & RAGS TO RICHES NOVELS

In 1886, the Statue of Liberty was dedicated by President Grover Cleveland to welcome the millions of immigrants wanting to achieve the American Dream.

They were from different countries and different denominations, notably Anglicans, Calvinists, Baptists, Dutch Reformed, Presbyterian, Methodists, Quakers, Lutherans, Moravians, Catholic and Jewish.

These newcomers had a "can do" attitude, to learn a new language, acquire new skills, engage in trade, accumulate hard earned wealth, and be charitable.

Immigrants were not a financial burden on taxpayers as there were no government welfare programs. Extended families and churches, both Protestant and Catholic, provided them welfare.

Their attitude was what German sociologist Max Weber described in *The Protestant Ethic and the Spirit of Capitalism,* 1904–1905, tracing how today's modern capitalism evolved from the hard-working Christians of Northern Europe who emphasized self-discipline, frugality, thrift, and avoidance of all forms of indulgence.

A genre of "rags to riches." Literature shared stories of impoverished immigrants, demonstrating the Christian work ethic and "American ingenuity," rose from humble beginnings, overcame adversity, achieved success and made contributions to society.

British educational writer Edward Hickson, editor of the *Westminster Review*, published a poem in *The Singing Master* in 1836, an excerpt of which was popularized in American author Thomas H Palmer's *Teacher's Manual,* 1840:

'Tis a lesson you should heed:

Try, try again.

If at first you don't succeed,

Try, try again.

Orison Swett Marden wrote *Pushing to the Front* in 1894, which was an instant best-seller, and founded *SUCCESS magazine* in 1897, which published inspirational stories of success in life through common-sense principles and well-rounded virtues.

Another best-selling author was Horatio Alger, who attended Harvard while Henry Wadsworth Longfellow was a professor there. He graduated in 1852, a member of Phi Beta Kappa, and in 1860, graduated from Harvard Divinity School.

When thousands of vagrant children flooded New York City, Alger wrote "rags to riches" novels to encourage street boys to rehabilitate their lives through hard work, perseverance, self-discipline, a positive attitude, an education, while shunning laziness, wrongdoing, and indulgence.

His "rags to riches" novels were read so widely that they had a formative effect on the United States from 1868 to 1899. They gave hope to millions, that no matter how bad someone's circumstances are, it is possible for them to achieve the American Dream.

Horatio Alger wrote over 100 books, which

by 1926, sold 20 million copies. His books warned of the dangers of vice and immorality and challenged young readers to hard work.

Alger's most popular novels were *Ragged Dick,* 1868; *Strong and Steady, or Paddle Your Own Canoe,* 1871; and *Shifting for Himself, or Gilbert Greyson's Fortune,* 1876.

Some noteworthy lines from his novels are:

> "Success in life is not measured by what you accomplish, but by the obstacles you overcome."

> "Success does not mean the absence of failure; it means the attainment of ultimate objectives."

> "There is nothing more powerful than honesty, and nothing more valuable than integrity."

> "There is no royal road to learning; it comes only through persevering effort, hard work, and constant self-improvement."

> "It is not wealth or rank, but virtue alone, that can make a man great."

> "Your destiny is not determined by your circumstances, but by your choices."

> "The only failure one should fear is not hugging to the purpose they see as best."

> "Opportunities don't happen. You create them."

"The best way to predict the future is to create it."

"The future belongs to those who believe in the beauty of their dreams."

"Believe you can and you're halfway there."

"The surest way to achieve success is to act as if it was already within your grasp."

"Fortunes gravitate to men whose minds have a clear vision of great ends."

"Courage, my boy! Your fortune is a sure thing."

"A boy cannot be estimated by what he once was, but by what he has the power to become."

"So long as there is life, hope is never absent."

"It is better to aim high and miss than to aim low and hit."

"He who is true to his profession, true to his fellow-men, and true to himself, should be sought out wherever men are gathered together."

"No character, however upright, is rightly understood until it has been revealed by a trial of temptation."

"It is not strange that success in youth should often end in failure; for youth is too often a season of over-confidence and inexperience."

"The love of money is the root of all evil."

"No duty is more pressing than that of returning thanks."

"The greatest secret of success is to know how to get along with people."

"The only way to do great work is to love what you do."

"Success is not final, failure is not fatal: It is the courage to continue that counts."

"The only thing standing between you and your goal is the story you keep telling yourself."

"Success is not in what you have, but who you are."

"The institution of chivalry forms one of the most remarkable features in the history of the Middle Ages."

Horatio Alger's novel *Ragged Dick* begins with a 14-year-old homeless orphan named Dick Hunter. When asked about his parents, he replied:

"I ain't got no mother. She died when I wasn't but three years old. My father went to sea; but he went off before mother died, and nothing' was ever heard of him.

I expect he got wrecked, or died at sea."

"And what became of you when your mother died?"

"The folks she boarded with took care of me, but they were poor, and they couldn't do much. When I was seven the woman died, and her husband went out West, and then I had to scratch for myself"

Alger described:

> He was above doing anything mean or dishonorable. He would not steal, or cheat, or impose upon younger boys, but was frank and straight-forward, manly and self-reliant. His nature was a noble one and had saved him from all mean faults.

In *Slow And Sure: The Young Street-Merchant,* 1872, Alger included the lines:

> "I shall be satisfied with less," said his mother. "Wealth alone will not yield happiness."
> "Still it is very comfortable to have it."
> "No doubt, if it is properly acquired."
> "If I am ever rich, mother, you may be sure that I shall not be ashamed of the manner in which I became so."

Mr. Greyson invited Dick to church. Dick put other's before himself, helping a homeless boy, Johnny Nolan get food; a shoe shine boy, Henry Fosdick, get lodging; and helping Tom Wilkins and his mother who were being evicted.

Someone commented on Dick's ragged clothes, to which he wittily gave a good-natured response:

> This coat once belonged to General Washington ... He wore it all through

> the Revolution, and it got torn some, cause he fit so hard ... if you'd like it, sir, to remember General Washington by, I'll let you have it reasonable.

He humorously persuaded customers to hire him to shine their shoes:

> I have to pay such a big rent for my manshun up on Fifth Avenoo, that I can't afford to take less than ten cents a shine.

Alger described Dick as being industrious in his bootblack job:

> He looked sharply in the faces of all who passed, addressing each with, "Shine yer boots, sir?"

Alger wrote:

> If his employment is an honest one, it is an honorable one.

After Dick earned enough money from four customers, he went to a shanty restaurant to buy some food. He continued to jump at every opportunity to get ahead, explaining to his unsuccessful friend Johnny:

> I keep my eyes open, — that's the way I get jobs. You're lazy, that's what's the matter.

Alger added:

> The difference between the rich merchant and the ragged fellow ... consists, frequently, not in natural ability, but in the fact that the one has used his ability as a stepping-stone to success.

Alger wrote:

> The boots were soon polished in Dick's best style, which proved very satisfactory, our hero being proficient in the art.

Alger gave dialogue of life on the streets:

> The rowdy looked at the boy who confronted him. Edward was slightly smaller, but there was a determined look in his eye which the bully, who, like those of his class generally, was a coward at heart, did not like. He mentally decided that it would be safer not to provoke him.

Alger added:

> I hope my young readers will not infer that I am an advocate of fighting. It can hardly help being brutal under any circumstances; but where it is never resorted to except to check ruffianism, as in the case of my young hero, it is less censurable.

Dick's hard work prepared him to take advantage of opportunities. His good character, straight-forward manner, and frank speech cause people to trust him. Alger wrote:

> Some of his companions were sly, and their faces inspired distrust; but Dick had a frank, straight-forward manner that made him a favorite.

One day, he overheard a busy businessman, Mr. Whitney, mentioning that he was looking for someone to give his nephew, Frank Whitney, a tour of New York City. Alger wrote:

> Now Dick had listened to all this conversation. Being an enterprising young man, he thought he saw a chance

for a speculation, and determined to avail himself of it.

Accordingly he stepped up to the two just as Frank's uncle was about leave, and said, "I know all about the city, sir; I'll show him around, if you want me to."

Mr. Whitney saw Dick's honesty and paid him five dollars to show Frank around.

Dick gave Frank a whirlwind tour of the city, showing him Trinity Church, the Barnum Museum, and Central Park, which was still being constructed. As they went down Fifth Street, the finest street in the city, Dick confessed that though needy, he refused to be a thief.

Dick told Frank that he has aspirations:

> I'd like to be a office boy, and learn business, and grow up spectable.

Dick had been sleeping on the street, so he used the five dollars he was paid for giving the city tour to rent a room at the News Boys Lodging House on Mott Street, paying 75 cents a day. The house was subsidized by New York businessmen, including Theodore Roosevelt's father.

> "It's the News-boys' Lodgin' House, on Fulton Street," said Dick, "up over the 'Sun' office. It's a good place. I don't know what us boys would do without it. They give you supper for six cents, and a bed for five cents more."
>
> "I suppose some boys don't even have the five cents to pay,–do they?"
>
> "They'll trust the boys," said Dick.

The conversation turned to entertainment:

> "It is the first fashionable party I ever attended."
>
> "Well," said Dick, "I haven't attended many. When I was a boot-black I found it interfered with my business, and so I always declined all the fashionable invitations I got."

His street smarts kept him from being duped, yet he was modest enough to admit he did not have the manners required in "genteel "society. Frank told him:

> A good many distinguished men have once been poor boys. There's hope for you Dick, if you'll try.

Frank advised him:

> You began in the right way when you determined never to steal, or to do anything mean or dishonorable, however strongly tempted to do so. That will make people have confidence in you when they come to know you.
>
> But, in order to succeed well, you must manage to get as good an education as you can.

Dick determined to pursue self-improvement, as Alger wrote:

> Dick had perseverance, and was not easily discouraged. He had made up his mind he must know more, and was not disposed to complain of the difficulty of the task.

Being illiterate, Dick arranged for his homeless orphan friend, Henry Fosdick, to stay free at the room he was renting in exchange for Henry teaching him the 3 R's – Reading, wRiting, and aRithmetic:

> "Then I'll tell you what," said Dick; "I'll make a bargain with you. I can't read much more'n a pig; and my writin' looks like hens' tracks.
> I don't want to grow up knowin' no more'n a four-year-old boy. If you'll teach me readin' and writin' evenin's, you shall sleep in my room every night.
> That'll be better'n door-steps or old boxes, where I've slept many a time."

His dream of becoming "spectable" was getting closer. Alger wrote:

> Dick had gained something more valuable than money. He had studied regularly every evening, and his improvement had been marvelous.
> He could now read well, write a fair hand, and had studied arithmetic ... Besides this, he had obtained some knowledge of grammar and geography.

Mr. Whitney and Frank got Dick some second-hand clothes to replace his ragged outfit, and took him to Astor House hotel where he could get cleaned up. Alger wrote:

> When Dick was dressed in his new attire, with his face and hands clean, and his hair brushed, it was difficult to imagine that he was the same boy.
> He now looked quite handsome, and might readily have been taken for a young gentleman, except that his hands were red and grimy.

"Look at yourself," said Frank, leading him before the mirror. "By gracious!" said Dick, starting back in astonishment, "that isn't me, is it?" "Don't you know yourself?" asked Frank, smiling

One afternoon, Dick and Henry Fosdick were taking the South Ferry. A father, Mr. Rockwell, went into a panic when his six-year-old boy fell into the river. As the boy was sinking, Dick, who knew how to swim, jumped in fully clothed and saved the boy.

The grateful father thanked Dick. Alger wrote:

> Our hero was ready enough to speak on most occasions, but always felt awkward when he was praised."

The father inquired about Dick's circumstances, and when he discovered he had educated himself to read and calculate, he hired him as a clerk for his business, paying him the large sum of ten dollars a week.

His hard work paid off. Young ragged Dick was transformed from a homeless street boy to a respectable clerk with a promising future.

Alger wrote:

> "Dick may have been lucky," said Mr. Rockwell, "but I generally find that luck comes oftenest to those who deserve it. If you will try to raise yourself I will help you."

This story of Horatio Alger, and many like it, was the lure for immigrants to come to the New World to achieve the American Dream.

Ragged Dick's story echoed that of the life of Benjamin Franklin, the tenth son of a Boston candle-maker, who worked hard, educated himself, and became successful.

Ben Franklin wrote in his *Autobiography:*

> I thence considered industry as a means of obtaining wealth and distinction which encouraged me – though I did not think that I should ever literally stand before kings, which, however, has since happened; for I have stood before five, and even had the honor of sitting down with one, the King of Denmark, to dinner.

In *The Autobiography,* Franklin listed virtues he sought to incorporate into his daily life:

> Temperance, Silence, Order, Resolution, Frugality, Industry, Sincerity, Justice, Moderation, Cleanliness, Tranquility, Chastity, and Humility.

Franklin advised:

> Lose no time; be always employed in something useful; cut off all unnecessary actions.

Horatio Alger remarked on history:

> The institution of chivalry forms one of the most remarkable features in the history of the Middle Ages ...
>
> Thus the castle of each feudal chieftain became a school of chivalry, into which any noble youth, whose parents were from poverty unable to educate him to the art of war, was

readily received ...
The candidate was required to prepare himself by confession, fasting, and passing the night in prayer.

Horatio Alger, convinced that anyone could achieve the American Dream, created characters who overcame hardship through industry, perseverance, self-reliance, and self-discipline.

In 1883, Horatio Alger published *Abraham Lincoln, the Backwoods Boy Or, How a Young Rail-splitter Became President.*

A notable comment by Lincoln in 1864 was:

> I happen temporarily to occupy this big White House. I am a living witness that anyone of your children may look to come here as my father's child has.
>
> It is in order that each of you may have through this free government which we have enjoyed, an open field and a fair chance for your industry, enterprise, and intelligence; that you may all have equal privileges in the race of life, with all its desirable human aspirations.
>
> It is for this, the struggle should be maintained, that we may not lose our birthright ... The nation is worth fighting for, to secure such an inestimable jewel.

BILLY SUNDAY, BASEBALL PLAYER TURNED PREACHER

Billy Sunday was born during the Civil War in a log cabin in Iowa. His father, who was a Union Army soldier, died of pneumonia when Billy was a month old. He wrote in his autobiography, "I never saw my father."

During his childhood, ten of his close relatives died. Poverty led his mother to send him and his siblings to the Soldier's Orphans Home.

At age 15, Billy Sunday struck out on his own, working several jobs before playing baseball.

His career took off when he was recruited by A.G. Spalding, owner of the Chicago White Stockings and founder of Spalding Sporting Goods Company. Billy Sunday played for the White Stockings and then the Philadelphia Phillies.

While leaving a Chicago saloon with some other players in 1886, he heard a group of Gospel singers on the street from the Pacific Garden Mission. Billy Sunday was attracted by the hymns, as they were the same ones his mother used to sing when he was a child.

While attending services at the mission he experienced a conversion. Billy began attending Y.M.C.A. meetings and quit drinking. That same year, he went to Jefferson Park Presbyterian Church where he was introduced to Helen Amelia "Nell" Thompson.

Her father disapproved of their relationship, as he considered baseball players "transient ne'er-do-wells who were unstable and destined to be misfits once they were too old to play."

Her father finally relented and gave his blessing. Billy and Nell were married September 5, 1888. Nell encouraged Billy, who was naturally shy, to begin speaking. She went on to organize his evangelistic meetings. He admitted he "never yet gone contrary to Mrs. Sunday's advice."

Billy Sunday gave up making $5,000 a year as a professional baseball player to working at the Y.M.C.A. for $75 a month.

On February 17, 1889, a national sensation occurred when 27-year-old Billy Sunday came out as a Christian evangelist, preaching his first sermon in Chicago. The press reported in sport terms:

> Center fielder Billy Sunday made a three-base hit at Farwell Hall last night. There is no other way to express the success of his first appearance as an evangelist in Chicago.
>
> His audience was made up of about 500 men who didn't know much about his talents as a preacher but could remember his galloping to second base with his cap in hand.

During the next 46 years, till his death November 6, 1935, over 100 million people heard Billy Sunday preach the Gospel through large-scale revival meetings and radio preaching.

His preaching was in the tradition of:

•Scotland revivals beginning in the 1730s;

•First Great Awakening preaching of George Whitefield;

•Second Great Awakening camp meetings and

preaching of Charles Finney;
- 1857 Pre-Civil War Layman's Prayer Revival begun by Jeremiah Lamphier;
- Post-Civil War evangelist D.L. Moody; and
- Welsh revivals at the turn of the last century.

Billy Sunday proclaimed in Des Moines, Iowa, November 3, 1914:

> When may a revival be expected? When the wickedness of the wicked grieves and distresses the Christian ...
>
> What a spell the devil seems to cast over the church today! ... If the church was down on her face in prayer they would be more concerned with the fellow outside. The church has degenerated into a third-rate amusement joint ...
>
> It is as much the duty of the church to awaken ... men and women of this city as it is the duty of the fire department to arouse when the call sounds.
>
> What would you think of the fire department of Des Moines if it slept while the town burned? You would condemn them and I will condemn you if you sleep and let men and women go to hell ...

Sunday added:

> Christians have lost the spirit of prayer ... Religion needs a baptism of horse sense ... If you go to a farmer and say ... God will give you crops only when it pleases him and it is no use for you plow your ground ... That is all wrong ...
>
> Revival may be expected when Christian people confess and ask forgiveness for their sins ...

> Break up your fallow ground ... Stand up and let people know you stand for Jesus Christ ...
>
> When may a revival be expected? ... When ... ministers ... thought they would die unless a revival would come to awaken their people, their students, their deacons, and their Sunday school workers, unless they would fall down on their faces and renounce the world and the works and deceits of the devil ...
>
> A revival ... returns the church from her backsliding and ... causes the conversion of man and women; and it always includes the conviction of sin ... A revival helps to bring the unsaved to Jesus Christ.

Billy Sunday preached on prayer:

> The man who truly prays "Thy kingdom come" cannot pass a saloon and not ask himself the question,
>
> "What can I do to get rid of that thing that is blighting the lives of thousands of young men, that is wrecking homes, and that is dragging men and women down to hell?"
>
> You cannot pray "Thy kingdom come," and then rush to the polls and vote for the thing that is preventing that kingdom from coming. You cannot pray "Thy kingdom come" and then go and do the things that make the devil laugh.
>
> For the man who truly prays "Thy kingdom come" it would be impossible to have one kind of religion on his knees and another when he is behind the counter; it would be impossible to have one kind of

religion in the pew and another in politics.
When a man truly prays "Thy kingdom come" he means it in everything or in nothing.

Billy Sunday's preaching against alcohol led to the passage of the 18th Amendment. He stated:

> I am the sworn, eternal, uncompromising enemy of the Liquor Traffic. I ask no quarter and I give none. I have drawn the sword in defense of God, home, wife, children and native land.

In 1910, Sunday preached a historic revival in Joplin, Missouri, a mining town known for hotels, women of the night, gambling and saloons. Rev. Frank Neff of Kansas Citys Independence Avenue Methodist Episcopal Church and president of the Ministers Alliance of Joplin, told reporters:

> We expect a great clean up in the city, but it will be in the nature of a religious awakening which will result in a permanent clean up and will come from a sincere desire of the people.

During Joplin's "Fifty Days of Sunday," Billy Sunday explained:

> A revival is the conviction of sin. Inside the church there must be a spiritual revival before it gets outside.

In his animated style, Billy Sunday said:

> Temptation is the devil looking through the keyhole. Yielding is opening the door and inviting him in.

Billy Sunday warned not to remove the Bible from public schools:

> Rivers of America will run with blood filled to their banks before we will submit to them taking the Bible out of our schools.

Billy Sunday inspired famous tent evangelists and revival preachers, such as Billy Graham, T.L. Osborne, Aimee Semple McPherson, Oral Roberts, Jimmy Swaggart, James Robison, Pat Robertson, Robert Schuller, Luis Palau, Reinhard Bonnke, Franklin Graham, and many more.

Ministry magazine published the article "Charles G. Finney–Prototype of the Modern Evangelist," November, 1976:

> It has been said "evangelism entered modernity with him." It was Finney who originated many of the methods used by such famous revivalists as Moody, Chapman, and Mills, who in turn passed them on to be adapted later by men such as Billy Sunday and Billy Graham.

Billy Sunday spoke in city after city across America. Tens of thousands heard him in month long meetings. Huge wooden auditoriums called "Billy Sunday Tabernacles" were built to accommodate the crowds. The floor was just the ground, so sawdust was put down to keep it from becoming muddy. When people answered the altar calls and came forward for prayer, Billy Sunday called it "walking the sawdust trail."

The Billy Sunday Tabernacle in Winona was the largest auditorium in northern Indiana for many years, seating 7,500. A Billy Sunday museum is on the campus of Grace College and Seminary in Winona Lake, Indiana.

Through his large-scale revival meetings and radio preaching, Billy Sunday presented the Gospel to an estimated 100 million people.

Billy Sunday's pioneering of Gospel radio birthed conservative talk radio. Other early broadcasting preachers included: Paul Rader, pastor of Moody Church, Chicago; Charles Fuller, founder of Fuller Theological Seminary; Aimee Semple McPherson, founder of the Foursquare Church; William Ward Ayer, pastor of Calvary Baptist Church in Manhattan; Walter A. Maier, The Lutheran Hour; Donald Grey Barnhouse, The Bible Study Hour; "Fighting Bob" Shuler; and Father Charles Coughlin.

Religious radio stations were initially unregulated and sometimes their powerful signals overlapped sports broadcasts, and occasionally they aired programing critical of politicians. This resulted in government regulating radio in 1926 by the FRC (Federal Radio Commission), which became the FCC in 1934.

In typical fashion, after the government began licensing, it began regulating, then revoking licenses, as it did to the popular radio broadcaster "Fighting Bob" Shuler in 1934, who was a national folk hero for exposing government corruption.

Teaching that salvation was through faith in Jesus Christ, not in organized religion, Billy Sunday explained that churches were fine so far as they were "in the world, but all wrong when the world is in them," adding:

> "You can go to hell just as fast from the church door as from the grog shop or bawdy house."

"Going to church doesn't make you a Christian any more than going to a garage makes you an automobile."

He assured believers of God's forgiveness:

"The devil says I'm out, but the Lord says I'm safe."

Billy Sunday stated:

I never see a man or a woman or boy or girl but I do not think that God has a plan for them ... He will use each of us to His glory if we will only let Him.

He challenged:

Live so that when the final summons comes you will leave something more behind you than an epitaph on a tombstone

⚘

HARVEST IS PLENTIFUL, LABORERS ARE FEW

The Salvation Army, the Y.M.C.A. and other charitable Christian organizations, were clear in presenting the life-changing Gospel:

"For whosoever shall call upon the name of the Lord shall be saved." (Romans 10:13)

"Jesus answered and said unto them, 'This is the work of God: that ye believe in Him whom He hath sent.'" (John 6:29)

> "For by grace you have been saved through faith, and that not of yourselves; it is the gift of God, not of works, lest anyone should boast." (Ephesians 2:8–9)

In addition, there are Scriptures which encourage believers to join in the work of sharing God's plan of salvation with others, to be His hands and feet on the earth, to let His will be carried out through them by doing loving works:

> "The harvest truly is plentiful, but the laborers are few. Therefore pray the Lord of the harvest to send out laborers into His harvest." (Matthew 9:37–38; Luke 10:2)

> "For the kingdom of heaven is like a landowner who went out early in the morning to hire laborers for his vineyard." (Matthew 20:1)

> "Now he who plants and he who waters are one, and each one will receive his own reward according to his own labor." (1 Corinthians 3:8)

> "Be steadfast, immovable, always abounding in the work of the Lord, knowing that your labor is not in vain in the Lord." (1 Corinthians 15:58)

> "I labored more abundantly than they all, yet not I, but the grace of God which was with me." (1 Corinthians 15:10)

> "To this end I also labor, striving according to His working which works in me mightily." (Colossians 1:29)

"Are they ministers of Christ?—I speak as a fool—I am more: in labors more abundant, in stripes above measure, in prisons more frequently, in deaths often." (2 Corinthians 11:23)

"... in stripes, in imprisonments, in tumults, in labors, in sleeplessness, in fastings ... "(2 Corinthians 6:5)

"And we labor, working with our own hands." (1 Corinthians 4:12)

"For you remember, brethren, our labor and toil; for laboring night and day, that we might not be a burden to any of you, we preached to you the Gospel of God." (1 Thessalonians 2:9)

"I have shown you in every way, by laboring like this, that you must support the weak." Acts 20:35

"Let us not grow weary while doing good, for in due season we shall reap if we do not lose heart." (Galatians 6:9)

"For God is not unjust to forget your work and labor of love." (Hebrews 6:10)

"For we are his workmanship, created in Christ Jesus for good works." (Ephesians 2:10)

WILLIAM BOOTH FOUNDED THE SALVATION ARMY

In 1902, President Theodore Roosevelt had lunch with William Booth, who had traveled to the U.S. Booth opened the Senate with prayer, as he had done four years earlier with President William McKinley.

Booth telegrammed Roosevelt, March 7, 1903:

> I am more than impressed with the greatness of the Nation at whose head you have been placed by the Providence of God. I pray that He may spare you all the wisdom needed ...
>
> These kindly feelings which you are known to entertain towards those who grow in misery and helplessness even in this greatly favored country ...
>
> May the blessing of Him that maketh rich and addeth no sorrow be on the White House and the Nation it represents."

William Booth was born April 10, 1829. At the age of 13, he was sent to apprentice as a pawnbroker, a job which made him aware of the humiliation and degradation that poor people suffered.

Becoming a Christian as a teenager, Booth studied the writings of Second Great Awakening preacher Charles Finney, particularly on the subject of revival. Booth began to boldly share his faith with others.

William married Catherine Mumford in 1855. As a child she had a spinal condition and tuberculosis which confined he to bed where she read through the Bible eight times and Charles Finney's *Revival Lectures.*

Both being 26-years-old, William and Catherine founded The Christian Revival Society, renamed Salvation Army, to preach the Gospel of Salvation, and minister to the poor, drunk, outcast, and wretched who lived in the dirty, dangerous slums of London's East End.

They fought to end child-trafficking and teenage prostitution. Catherine Booth said:

> I felt as though I must go and walk the streets and besiege the dens where these hellish iniquities are going on. To keep quiet seemed like being a traitor to humanity.

With the help of Josephine Butler, they pressured politicians to pass England's Criminal Law Amendment Act in 1885, raising the age of consent from 13 to 16.

In 1884, The Salvation Army established London's first rescue home for women and girls, and in the next 30 years, had 117 homes around the world. Booth wrote:

> While women weep, as they do now, I'll fight;
> –while little children go hungry, I'll fight;
> –while men go to prison, in and out, in and out, as they do now, I'll fight;
> –while there is a drunkard left,
> –while there is a poor lost girl upon the streets,
> –where there remains one dark soul without the light of God — I'll fight! I'll fight to the very end!

Embracing the "spiritual army" concept, they

adopted semi-military uniforms and regimented system of leadership. Before long, they had 81 mission stations staffed by 127 full-time evangelists, coordinating over 1,900 voluntary speakers, holding 75,000 meetings a year.

In 1881, Catherine Booth–Clibborn, the oldest daughter of William and Catherine Booth, brought The Salvation Army to Switzerland and France, against local opposition.

In 1885, The Salvation Army began operating in the United States, and has since worked in 134 countries, with 1.7 million members, ministering to "physical and spiritual needs" of an estimated 30 million a year in shelters, charity shops, disaster relief and humanitarian aid.

Booker T. Washington, founder of the Tuskegee Institute, replied to a letter from Major T.C. Marshall, editor of The Salvation Army's *Conqueror Magazine*, July 28, 1896:

> I am very glad to hear that The Salvation Army is going to undertake work among my people in the southern states.
>
> I have always had the greatest respect for the work of The Salvation Army especially because I have noted that it draws no color line in religion ...
>
> In reaching the neglected and, I might say, outcasts of our people, I feel that your methods and work have peculiar value ...
>
> God bless you in all your unselfish Christian work for our country.

Booth is credited with saying:

> Most Christian organizations would like to send their workers to Bible

college for five years. I would like to send our workers to Hell for five minutes. That would prepare them for a lifetime of compassionate ministry.

On June 24, 1904, Booth met King Edward the VII at Buckingham Palace. When the King asked what his recreations were, Booth responded:

Sir, some men have a passion for art, fame and gold. I have a passion for souls.

Once asked what was the secret of his success, he replied:

I will tell you the secret. God has had all there was of me. There have been men with greater brains than I, men with greater opportunities.

But from the day I got the poor of London on my heart and caught a vision of all Jesus Christ could do with them, on that day I made up my mind that God would have all of William Booth there was.

And if there is anything of power in the Salvation Army today, it is because God has had all the adoration of my heart, all the power of my will, and all the influence of my life.

He declared:

We must wake ourselves up! Or somebody else will take our place and bear our cross, and thereby rob us of our crown.

William Booth met with Winston Churchill. He was awarded London's Badge of Honor and an honorary degree from Oxford.

Booth died August 20, 1912. Over 150,000

people viewed his casket with 40,000 attending his funeral, with England's royalty sending their respects. At his Memorial Service, messages were read from the King and Queen, President William Taft, the German Emperor, John Wanamaker, Cardinal Gibbons, and Theodore Roosevelt.

Reverend L.L. Ritchie gave the eulogy:

> The one great characteristic of the General was his dauntless faith. No such word as impossible was in his vocabulary, for he knew it was not in God's dictionary.

William Booth stated:

> The chief danger of the 20th century will be religion without the Holy Ghost, Christianity without Christ, forgiveness without repentance, salvation without regeneration, politics without God, and Heaven without Hell.

Booth wrote:

> What are you living for? What is the deep secret purpose that controls and fashions your existence? What do you eat and drink for?
>
> What is the end of your marrying and giving in marriage – your money – making and toilings and plannings?
>
> Is it the salvation of souls, the overthrow of the kingdom of evil, and the setting up of the Kingdom of God?
>
> If not, you may be religious ... but I don't see how you can be a Christian.

THE GIDEONS BEGAN IN A Y.M.C.A.

In 1898, businessman John H. Nicholson arrived at the Central Hotel at Boscobel, Wisconsin, only to find it was overbooked.

As was the custom of the day, the innkeeper offered him a double room with another businessman, Samuel E. Hill. Discovering they both believed in Jesus, they had a Bible study and prayer time.

Sensing the Holy Spirit had ordered their steps, within a year they called a meeting July 1, 1899, at the Y.M.C.A in Janesville, Wisconsin, where they established the Gideons International, the oldest Association of Christian business and professional men in the United States of America.

In 1908, Archie Bailey placed a Bible in a hotel in Superior, Montana. Since then 269,500 Gideons and Auxiliary in 200 countries have distributed over 2 billion Bibles and New Testaments in hotels, hospitals, the military and schools.

⁂

BOOKER T. WASHINGTON FOUNDED TUSKEGEE

Booker T. Washington graduated from the Hampton Institute in Virginia. At the age of 25, he traveled to Alabama and founded Tuskegee Normal and Industrial Institute on July 4, 1881, with 37 students, meeting in the Butler Chapel

African Methodist Episcopal Zion Church.

The next year, he purchased land where students made bricks and built the first buildings. During his tenure, the school grew to over 2,000 students and a faculty of 200 teaching 40 trades.

Washington became one of the most significant figures in post-Reconstruction America, authoring 14 books, the most famous being *Up From Slavery*.

He described life at Tuskegee being filled with Sunday preaching services, Sunday school classes, daily evening chapel devotionals and a "Week of Prayer" held two weeks every January.

Students cared for the sick, needy, and elderly in the area, helped out at community churches, ran a Y.M.C.A., and staffed a Humane Society for the care of animals.

Washington wrote in *Up From Slavery*, 1901:

> While a great deal of stress is laid upon the industrial side of the work at Tuskegee, we do not neglect or overlook in any degree the religious and spiritual side.
>
> The school is strictly undenominational, but it is thoroughly Christian, and the spiritual training of the students is not neglected.
>
> Our preaching service, prayer meetings, Sunday school, Christian Endeavor Society, Young Men's Christian Association, and various missionary organizations testify to this.

The Booker T. Washington Papers, Vol. 5: 1899–1900 (Illinois University Press, 1976) recorded Washington's address at Memorial Hall in Columbus, Ohio, May 24, 1900:

> Dr. Washington walked on the stage at Memorial Hall with a firm, confident tread, as one sure of his ground ... His shoulders are broad and six feet of stature gives strength and poise to command respect. His hair is close cut and gives him the aspect of a war dog with all its tenacious fighting spirit.
>
> The eyes, however, gleam with kindliness and they temper the appearance of the latent fighting forces ... His jaw has the firmness of one who has the courage to stand by his convictions ...
>
> It's easy to see how that man succeeds," whispered a delegate to the Bible students' conference after looking at the speaker ...

The description continued:

> John R. Mott, general secretary of the Y.M.C.A. student movement of North America, presided at the afternoon meeting at Memorial Hall ... Mr. Mott announced Dr. Washington's subject as "The Place of the Bible in the Uplifting of the Negro Race."

The description concluded:

> Dr. Washington began his address after a quartet sang. He spoke of the ninety-one Y.M.C.A. organizations for colored youths; of the 5000 colored men studying the Bible, and of the 640 Bible students at Tuskegee, and pointed these as living examples of the progress of the Negro. He pleaded for two more secretaries to teach Bible in the South-land.

Booker T. Washington began a Bible training school at Tuskegee in 1893:

> While the institution is in no sense denominational, we have a department known as the Phelps Hall Bible Training School, in which a number of students are prepared for the ministry and other forms of Christian work, especially work in the country districts.
>
> In the school we made a special effort to teach our students the meaning of Christmas, and to give them lessons in its proper observance ...
>
> The Season now has a new meaning, not only through all that immediate region, but ... wherever our graduates have gone.

Washington gave students advice:

> "There are two ways of exerting one's strength: one is pushing down, the other is pulling up."
>
> "The surest way to lift up ourselves, is to lift up someone else."
>
> "If you want to lift yourself up, lift up someone else."
>
> "A race, like an individual, lifts itself up by lifting others up."
>
> "There is no escape — man drags man down, or man lifts man up."
>
> "You can't hold a man down without staying down with him."

> "The happiest people are those who do the most for others. The most miserable are those who do the least."

> "Keep in mind that service to our fellows will always be our greatest protection, and will bring our greatest happiness."

> "The harder the work required on account of the ... unpopularity of the individual to be helped, the greater will be the strength and happiness gained."

> "Remember that the only way to show ourselves superior to others is to excel them in kindlier impulses and more generous deeds."

Washington became friends with the most renowned entrepreneurs and philanthropists of his day, including Andrew Carnegie, John D. Rockefeller, George Eastman, and William Howard Taft. Their donations funded his initiatives and programs aimed at educating African–Americans.

In 1900, Booker T. Washington founded the National Negro Business League, growing it to 600 chapters.

He stated:

> Anyone can seek a job, but it requires a person of rare ability to create a job ... What we should do in our schools is to turn out fewer job seekers and more job creators.

Harvard President Charles W. Eliot spoke at Tuskegee's 25th anniversary in 1906, stating:

> By 1905, Tuskegee produced more

self-made millionaires than Harvard, Yale and Princeton combined.

Inspired by the National Negro Business League supporting entrepreneurship, Taft created the U.S. Chamber of Commerce in 1912.

Booker T. Washington's solution of the "race problem" was to gain respect through economic independence – a path taken by every wave of immigrants.

German, Irish, Jewish, Polish, Italian, Asian, and other immigrants arrived at the bottom of the social ladder and were often met with racial discrimination. They would work hard, get educated, start businesses, and pool their resources. As they accumulated wealth and contributed to society, they rose in public respect.

Booker T. Washington stated:

> At the bottom ... there must be for our race, as for all races ... economic prosperity, economic independence ...
> Political independence disappears without economic independence.

He recommended that they:

> ... concentrate all their energies on industrial education, and accumulation of wealth, and the conciliation of the South ... (then) Blacks would eventually gain full participation in society by showing themselves to be responsible, reliable American citizens.

Washington expressed his views:

> In the sight of God there is no color line, and we want to cultivate a spirit

that will make us forget that there is such a line anyway.

He wrote in *Up From Slavery*, 1901:

> It is now long ago that I learned this lesson from General Samuel Chapman Armstrong, and resolved that I would permit no man, no matter what his color might be, to narrow and degrade my soul by making me hate him.
>
> With God's help, I believe that I have completely rid myself of any ill feeling toward the Southern white man for any wrong that he may have inflicted upon my race. I am made to feel just as happy now when I am rendering service to Southern white men as when the service is rendered to a member of my own race.
>
> I pity from the bottom of my heart any individual who is so unfortunate as to get into the habit of holding race prejudice.

He wrote in *The Story of My Life and Work*:

> I have long since ceased to cherish any spirit of bitterness against the Southern white people on account of the enslavement of my race.

Washington wrote in *Up From Slavery*, 1901:

> Great men cultivate love ... only little men cherish a spirit of hatred. I learned that assistance given to the weak makes the one who gives it strong; and that oppression of the unfortunate makes one weak.

Booker T. Washington referenced Abraham Lincoln in his address to the Republican Club of

New York City, February 12, 1909. He stated:

> One man cannot hold another man down in the ditch without remaining down in the ditch with him.

Booker T. Washington stated:

> Character, not circumstances, makes the man ... You may fill your heads with knowledge or skillfully train your hands, but unless it is based upon high upright character, upon a true heart, it will amount to nothing.

He wrote in *Sowing and Reaping* (Boston, 1900):

> Success or failure depends very largely upon the side of life we choose.
>
> Every person desires to choose either the higher or the lower side of life, and with the choice a determination is made to live for higher or for lower things.
>
> It is evident that: if a person chooses the higher side of life, and lives up to his choice, he will succeed; but, on the other hand, if he chooses the lower side of life he will fail. "The way of the transgressor is hard." There is no escape. We should always strive to see things from the higher-life point of view.
>
> Instead of picking flaws in the character, and making unjust and uncalled for criticisms upon our neighbors and their work, we should encourage them in order that they may improve. If there is any good in a person, let us seek to find it; the evil will take care of itself.
>
> One of the greatest temptations young people have, who live on the lower side of

life, is to engage in profane, vulgar, and boisterous conversation. The nature of a person's conversation largely determines what he is.

Young people especially should seek to converse with persons whose conversation, whose thought, is pure and refined. The influence of unhealthy conversation is so great that nothing can counteract the harm it does a person's character.

If a young person finds himself associated with a person of either sex who has no regard for healthy thinking and pure expression, he should rid himself of the association. If he does not do so, he will eventually fall to the level of his companion. It is true that "birds of a feather flock together."

Young as well as old people should avoid the habit of speaking ill of others. The person who is always talking about somebody else must necessarily possess a low and cowardly nature ...

The gossiper and vilifier usually gets the worst of it in the end. So, above all things, avoid the habit of talking about others.

Evil association is another thing that will injure the reputation of a person. Nothing is so likely to injure the reputation of a young person as associating with persons who are low and vulgar in their conduct and speech.

Young people, especially, should never associate with persons whose influence will drag them down. If their companionship is not a help it should be abandoned,

> because in all conditions of life "evil communications corrupt good manners."
>
> The tendency of our nature, at the very best, is downward. If we do not associate with the best people possible in our condition of life, shame and degradation will inevitably be our portion. We should seek always the companionship of people who live high and think high and act high.
>
> Show me a person who entertains high thoughts, endorses high actions, and who possesses a broad and generous nature, and I will show you a person who is respected and beloved by his neighbors.

At Memorial Hall in Columbus, Ohio, May 24, 1900, Booker T. Washington stated:

> The men doing the vital things of life are those who read the Bible and are Christians and not ashamed to let the world know it ... No man can read the Bible and be lazy.

FREDERICK DOUGLASS AND SELF-MADE MEN

Frederick Douglass, the Republican advisor to Lincoln, did not believe in "the good luck theory," attributing success to chance and circumstances. He believed a person succeeded by hard work, both physical and mental.

Douglass gave the commencement address at

Tuskegee, May 26, 1892, titled "Self-Made Men," a talk he had previously given in 1859 and 1872:

> Self-made men ... are the men who owe little or nothing to birth, relationship, friendly surroundings; to wealth inherited or to early approved means of education; who are what they are, without the aid of any of the favoring conditions by which other men usually rise in the world and achieve great results ...
>
> The man who will get up will be helped up; and the man who will not get up will be allowed to stay down ...
>
> My general answer is, give the Negro fair play and let him alone ...
>
> Where circumstances do most for men, there man will do least for himself ... His doing makes or unmakes him ... My theory of self-made men is, then, simply this; that they are men of work ...
>
> Honest labor faithfully, steadily and persistently pursued, is the best, if not the only, explanation of their success.

Douglass' views were similar to those of Swiss education pioneer Johann Heinrich Pestalozzi (1746-1827), who stated:

> "Whoever is unwilling to help himself can be helped by no one."
>
> "The greatest victory a man can win is victory over himself."

MARY KINNAIRD: YOUNG WOMEN'S CHRISTIAN ASSOC.

The Y.M.C.A. inspired Mary Jane Kinnaird a prominent woman in England, to co-found the Young Women's Christian Association in 1855.

Born in 1816, Mary Jane was raised as an orphan. She grew up reading the works of evangelist William Romaine, studied the Bible, and engaged in daily prayers and evangelism.

Her uncle was a Baptist pastor in London, whose name, oddly enough, was Baptist Wriothesley Noel. He ministered at St John's Chapel in Bedford Row, and gave a notable speech at the Exeter Hall Y.M.C.A.

At the age of 21, Mary Jane began working as her uncle's church secretary. In 1841, she established St John's Training School for Domestic Servants, and later founded the United Association for the Christian and Domestic Improvement of Young Women.

Wanting to spread European Protestantism, she and her uncle visited with French minister Frédéric Monod and Swiss minister Jean-Henri Merle d'Aubigné, and helped raise funds for a Calvin memorial hall in Geneva, Switzerland.

In 1843, she married Lord Arthur Kinnaird, a prominent banker. Together they had six children, five of which lived to adulthood. They funded many philanthropic works, missions, hospitals, and supported women's suffrage.

With a passion to help the people of India, she formed the Indian Female Normal School and

Instruction Society, founding over 60 schools, associated with 1,300 zenanas — women's homes.

In recognition of her generosity, a hospital and school in India were named for her, as well as a school in Lahore, Pakistan – the Kinnaird Christian Girls' High School. It grew to become Kinnaird College for Women.

Mary Jane Kinnaird had worked with Florence Nightingale to train nurses so they could care for soldiers during the Crimean War with Russia, 1853–1856. She provided a home in London where the nurses could stay as traveled to and from the war. The home even had its own library.

She fought "white slavery," where young girls were kidnapped into prostitution. She joined the efforts of William and Catherine Booth, founders of The Salvation Army, which resulted in the British government, in 1886, raising the age of consent from age 13 to 16.

In 1878, Mary Jane Kinnaird and Emma Robarts formed the Prayer Union, made up of hundreds of Bible study groups who worked with the Women's Emigration Society to assist women immigrants get jobs. The Prayer Union groups offer combined prayer for the salvation of women worldwide. This was the origin of the Y.W.C.A.– Young Women's Christian Association.

The Y.W.C.A. joined the Y.M.C.A. in a prayer emphasis, agreeing in 1901 "on the adoption of the same subjects for the annual Week of Prayer," as cited on The World Y.M.C.A.'s webpage "History of the Week of Prayer" (accessed 1/14/25).

In 1904, a joint call to prayer was issued by the World Y.W.C.A. and the World Alliance of

Y.M.C.A.s. The joint Week of Prayer continued, and beginning in 1927, included messages from the President of the World Y.W.C.A. and the President of the World Alliance of Y.M.C.A.s. In 1931, the name was changed to "The Week of Prayer and World Fellowship."

Since 1942, the World Y.W.C.A. and the World Alliance of Y.M.C.A.s jointly published an annual Week of Prayer booklet. Since 1948, the booklets were printed with pictures, daily messages, prayers and Bible verses.

Donald Fraser explained in *Mary Jane Kinnaird* (London: Nisbet & Co., 1890) that she championed a prayer movement for world evangelism, similar to the Y.M.C.A.s Week of Prayer. She wrote in a tract that believers should offer "... united prayer in reference ... to the condition of the Jews, Mohammedans, and the heathen world."

Kinnaird explained:

> Prayer ... awakens such strong opposition ... from the world, the flesh, and the devil ... Hence the power of prayer — when to one God and Father, through one Lord and Savior Jesus Christ, and by one Holy Spirit, the prompter of prayer, the multitude of them that believe appeal for ... strength to fight the good fight of faith.

DR. LUTHER H. GULICK, JR. & Y.M.C.A. TRIANGLE

"I pray God your whole spirit and soul and body be preserved blameless unto the coming of our Lord Jesus Christ." – 1 Thessalonians 5:23

Dr. Luther Halsey Gulick Jr., was born to medical missionary parents in Honolulu, Hawaiian Islands, on December 4, 1865.

The Historical Journal of Massachusetts (Vol. 39, Summer 2011) published historian Clifford Putney's article "Luther Gulick: His Contributions to Springfield College, the Y.M.C.A., and Muscular Christianity," in which he wrote:

> Luther's grandfather, Peter Gulick, got caught up in the evangelical fervor of the Second Great Awakening and decided to eschew farming in New Jersey for a career as a Presbyterian missionary.
>
> He sought employment from the American Board of Commissioners for Foreign Missions, the country's first creator of overseas Christian missions. It assigned him to the kingdom of Hawaii in 1827 ...
>
> The ABCFM expected its male missionaries to marry before they encountered seductive "heathen" women overseas and it made no exception for Luther's grandfather.
>
> Peter Gulick cast around for a wife and ended up marrying Fanny Thomas, the descendant of an old Connecticut family.

> She was a schoolteacher in New York who had been converted to Christianity in 1826 by Charles Grandison Finney, the greatest American evangelist of his day. Finney went on to lead Oberlin College, America's first biracial and coeducational school ...
>
> Peter and Fanny had eight children, starting with Luther (who will henceforth be referred to by his nickname, Halsey, to distinguish him from his son, the primary subject of this article) ...
>
> All were taught to believe in social equality and to abhor both slavery and the oppression of women.

Luther "Hasley" Gulick became a medical doctor and served with his wife, Louisa, as missionaries in Hawaii when their son, Luther Gulick, Jr. was born.

From 1880 to 1882, Luther Gulick, Jr., studied at Oberlin Academy, a preparatory branch of Oberlin College. His desire to study physical training led him to transfer to Sargent Normal School, now Boston University's College of Health and Rehabilitation Sciences, 1883–1886.

In 1887, he married Charlotte "Lottie" Emily Vetter of Hanover, New Hampshire, and in 1889, he graduated from New York University's Medical School.

At the age of 24, Gulick founded the department of physical education at Y.M.C.A.'s International Training School, in Springfield, Massachusetts (now Springfield College). He served as superintendent there from 1887 to 1900.

This became the headquarters of a missionary

movement which sent thousands of Y.M.C.A. missionaries around the world. Athletic outreach drew many young men to be trained in sports but also in the Gospel.

Athletics at the Y.M.C.A. were primarily calisthenics and gymnastics.

In the 1880s, a devout Baptist named Robert J. Roberts was Physical Education Director at the Boston Y.M.C.A. He pioneered the fitness movement and advanced physical education as a profession. He recommended every person make exercise part of their daily routine. He led aerobics-style fitness drills and exercise classes using wooden dumbbells, heavy medicine balls, and Indian Clubs – a type of long-necked bowling pin. Roberts coined the term "body-building" and published a book in 1916 titled *The Body-Builder*.

Dr. Gulick believed gym instructors should also be soul winners. Students at the Y.M.C.A. International Training Center were required to take courses in:

> Bible History and Exegesis; The History of Evangelical Christianity; Christian Evidences; Old and New Testament Canon; Fundamental Doctrines of the Bible; Books of the Bible; Christian Ethics; Outline Study of Man; Practical Methods of Christian Work; Rules for Deliberative Bodies; Rhetoric and Logic; and Vocal Music.

Dormitory life had a monastic-like regimen:

6:00 am Rising Bell
6:15 to 7:00 Private devotion and preparation
 for the day's work

7:00 to 7:30 Breakfast
7:30 to 8:00 Walking in the open air
8:00 to 8:15 Put room in order
8:15 to 11:00 Study
11:00 to 12:00 Recitations
12:00 to 12:45 Instruction in gymnasium
1:00 to 1:30 Dinner
1:30 to 3:00 Study
3:00 to 5:00 Recitation
5:00 to 5:15 Evening prayer
5:15 to 6:00 Walking in open air or instruction in gymnasium
6:00 to 6:30 Supper
6:30 to 7:00 Rest
7:00 to 9:30 Study, reading and practical Christian work
10:30 Building closes and lights out.

Saturdays were devoted to recreation. On Sundays students were counseled to "avoid more than four engagements on the Sabbath," and, in all things, remember I Corinthians 10:13:

> "There hath no temptation taken you but such is common to man: but God is faithful, who will not suffer you to be tempted above that ye are able, but will with the temptation also make a way to escape, that ye may be able to bear it."

Once, when the weather was bitterly cold, Dr. Gulick asked Y.M.C.A. Instructor James Naismith to create a game which could be played indoors that would be more engaging than exercise drills.

In response, Naismith created "basketball." Gulick helped Naismith spread basketball to other Y.M.C.A.s around the world. It turned out to be an ideal evangelistic activity.

Y.M.C.A. missionaries in places as far away as France, India, Iran, China and Japan, would invite young men to play basketball and in the process develop relationships with them, invite them to Bible studies and prayer meetings, and then introduce them to Christ.

Sports became a way to recruit young men to church. In 1894, in London's poor East End, Anglican Reverend Arthur Osborne Montgomery Jay, of Holy Trinity Shoreditch Church, built a gymnasium with a boxing ring in the church's basement. He organized a boxing club, and when other churches followed, he hosted boxing tournaments.

In 1896, James Huff McCurdy arrived at the Y.M.C.A. Training Center in Springfield to be an assistant to Dr. Gulick. There, he introduced field hockey to the United States, codifying the rules in 1900.

James Naismith also created a less injury-prone version of football called "Team Ball," but it never caught-on.

Dr. Gulick chaired the Basketball Committee of the Amateur Athletic Union from 1895 to 1905.

At the 1904 World's Fair in St. Louis, he promoted physical exercise in schools. He directed the physical training of students in New York City's public schools from 1903 to 1908, being president of the Public School Physical Training Society in 1905–1908.

He represented the U.S. Olympic Committee at the Olympic Games in 1908.

From 1908 to 1913, he directed the Russell

Sage Foundation's child hygiene department, and was president of the American Physical Education Association in 1903–1906.

In 1907, he became president of the Playground Association of America, which became the National Recreation and Park Association.

Gulick founded a boys summer camp called Camp Timanous, and, with the help of his wife, founded a girls camp, Camp Wohelo.

When World War I started, he inspected U.S. Army troops in France, wearing his Y.M.C.A. red triangle logo. Upon his return, he unfortunately became ill and died, August 13, 1918, while visiting their Campfire Girls of America camp in Casco, Maine.

In 1959, Dr. Gulick was inducted into the Basketball Hall of Fame. He was awarded an Honorary Fellow in Memoriam by National Academy of Kinesiology.

Gulick and his wife are honored by one of 34 bronze plaques on The Extra Mile – Points of Light Volunteer Pathway adjacent to the White House in Washington D.C., a memorial to those who "through their caring and personal sacrifice, reached out to others, building their dreams into movements that helped people across America and throughout the world."

Historian Clifford Putney, author of *Muscular Christianity: Manhood and Sports in Protestant America 1880–1920* (Cambridge, MA: Harvard University Press, 2003) explained:

> He was the greatest of Y.M.C.A. philosophers ...

Before Gulick, the "Y" had kept gymnastics subordinate to evangelism.

After him, it held physical fitness, no less than religious conviction, responsible for leading men to Glory.

Dr. Gulick edited:

Physical Education (1891–1896);

Association Outlook (1897–1900);

American Physical Education Review (1901–1903); and

Gulick Hygiene Series — five textbooks for elementary school use on physiology and hygiene of body and mind, written in a narrative style to hold the interest of the pupil, especially as they relate to the student's own life and environment.

His books include:

Manual of Physical Measurements (1892);

Ten minutes' exercise for busy men: a complete course in physical education: five separate courses, free work, chest weights, dumb bells, wands, Indian clubs. American Sports Publishing Company, (1902);

Physical Education by Muscular Exercise (1904);

The Efficient Life (1907);

Mind and Work (1908);

The Healthful Art of Dancing (1910);

Medical Inspection of Schools, with Leonard Porter Ayres (1908, 1913); and

Health by Muscular Gymnastics (1916).

Dr. Gulick added the "Spirit–Mind–Body" triangle to the original Y.M.C.A. logo. This also became the seal of Springfield College.

The Y.M.C.A. of Central Florida website (accessed 1/18/25) has a page, *Spiritual Legacy – The Original Y.M.C.A. Logo:*

> Inside the circle are the first two letters of the word Christ. The Greek letters Chi and Rho (XP) form the ancient symbol that early Christians painted on the walls of the catacombs.
>
> It was used by the Y.M.C.A. to remind all that Christ was at the center of the movement.
>
> Finally, an open Bible was added, "both because this divine book is the weapon of warfare which St. John gives to young men, and because it's the distinguishing mark of the great Reformation.
>
> The Bible opens on the Savior's High Priestly prayer, from which we have especially chosen the 21st verse: 'That they all may be one...as We are one' –John 17:21." This remains the Y.M.C.A.'s official emblem.

The Chi and Rho "XP" were the first two Greek letters of the name of Christ — "Χριστοῦ."

Gulick explained in "What The Triangle Means, published in *Young Men's Era*, January 18, 1894, Number 3:

> The triangle stands ... for the man as a whole ... to indicate that the individual, while he may have different aspects, is a unit ...
>
> The triangle stands, not merely for symmetrical body, a symmetrical mind, a symmetrical character, but for the

symmetrical man, each part developed with reference to the whole ...

What authority have we for believing that this triangle idea is correct?

It is scriptural.

Deuteronomy 6:5, "And thou shalt love the Lord thy God with all thine heart, and with all thy soul, and with all thy might;"

2 Kings 23:25, "And like unto him was there no king before him, that turned to the Lord with all his heart, and with all his soul, and with all his might, according to the law of Moses: neither after him arose there any like him:" ...

Luke 10: 27, "And He answering said, Thou shalt love the Lord thy God with all thy heart, and with all thy soul, and with all thy strength, and with all thy mind, and thy neighbor as thyself; "

Dr. Gulick continued:

In each passage referring to what is involved in the service of the Lord, "heart" is always stated, but usually in connection with other elements.

Thus such statements ... indicate that the scriptural view is that the service of the Lord includes the whole man.

The words, which in the Hebrew and Greek are translated "strength," refer in both cases entirely to physical strength.

Then we are told that the body is a member of Christ.

> 1 Corinthians 6:15, "Know we not that your bodies are the members of Christ? Shall I, then, take the members of Christ, and make them the members of an harlot? God forbid:" — that it is "a temple of the Holy Ghost."
>
> 1 Corinthians 6:19. "What? know ye not that your body is the temple of the Holy Ghost which is in you, which ye have of God, and ye are not your own:" and that it is eternal,
>
> 1 Corinthians 15. This chapter deals very largely with the resurrection body ...
> We have the same scriptural warrant for believing that our physical characteristics will endure to eternity as we have for believing that our character will be immortal. We shall carry into the next world the one, as well as the other ...

He added:

> The history of nations proves that physical welfare is always connected with the welfare of mind and spirit.
> In our own experience we know that times of physical depression often coincide with depression that is intellectual and spiritual ...
> Why should this emblem be adopted by the Young Men's Christian Association if it is a broad and generally accepted Truth?
> The Young Men's Christian Association is the only great institution of the world which, in a large way, is

putting this belief into actual practice.

It aims at the salvation and upbuilding of the whole man to a greater extent than does any other institution in the world, both in respect to unity and symmetry ...

It is by means of the physical that men are brought under the influence of the spiritual, and it is the spiritual that teaches men that their bodies are sacred to noble ends, and that the gymnasium is one of the means to the accomplishment of those ends.

We not only secure all that is of inherent value in our physical department, but by virtue of its relation to the others, we also secure that which is of far greater value, and thus the total of our results is greater than the sum of the results in each department

And so we have our gymnasiums and our educational classes, our libraries, reading-rooms, and our religious work, a unit in conception, a complete rounded whole, that is invaluable now, and gives promise of becoming, in the hands of God, the means of good far beyond our present thought.

Dr. Luther Gulick concluded:

All this is in line with the laws of God which we find not only in the Bible, but in science; in line with all that we are learning about man's nature, character and ultimate development, in line also with the still further perfecting of this wonderful, complete unit, this organism that God has put in our keeping ...

The various departments of the Young Men's Christian Association are coming to bear the same kind of relation to each other that the various parts of man do, so that the physical department is not a sort of separate institution off by itself, with different aims and ends, but is a part of the very institution itself, and in touch with the educational, spiritual and social lines of work, all aiming at the one thing, the salvation and up-building of the man.

Sometimes the triangle is criticized in that it does not stand for the social and economic lines of work of the Young Men's Christian Association. The answer is that the triangle does not stand for lines of work at all, but simply for the complete man ...

This conception of unity and symmetry we believe to be the most fundamental and distinctive fact of the Young Men's Christian Association.

LUTHER & LOTTIE GULICK FOUNDED CAMP FIRE GIRLS

Having been a part of both the Y.M.C.A. and the Boy Scouts, Dr. Luther Gulick and his wife Charlotte "Lottie" Gulick, founded in 1910 the nondenominational Camp Fire Girls.

Just as the Gulick's helped the Boy Scouts include exercise and physical fitness in their programs, they did the same for young women.

They modeled its symbol after the Y.M.C.A. triangle, emphasizing the development of the whole person — physical, mental, spiritual.

They encouraged cooperation with other groups, as stated in *The Book of the Camp Fire Girls*, 1914, in Chapter IV—"Meetings":

> Quite a number of Camp Fires give part of their time aiding other organizations, assisting in church fairs, helping the Boy Scouts to raise money, and visiting orphan's homes and other institutions.

The Book of the Camp Fire Girls, 1914, Chapter III—"Honors" included:

> Business: Yellow Honors ... Earn three dollars and give it to some philanthropic, church, or community interest ...
>
> Patriotism: Red, White and Blue Honors ... Teach a class of not less than three, once a week, for eight months in connection with a church, tabernacle, settlement, Young Women's Christian Association, Young Women's Hebrew Association, or other educational or social institution ...
>
> Attend a service ten Sabbaths in three months. Give brief accounts of the life and service of five religious leaders, and five missionaries ...
>
> Commit to memory the Preamble to the Constitution, Lincoln's Gettysburg Address, and the first two paragraphs of the Declaration of Independence.
>
> Commit to memory one hundred verses of the Bible or an equal amount of

other sacred literature, as hymns, Thomas à Kempis' *The Imitation of Christ*, etc.

Chapter II—"Membership, Rank and Names" of *The Book of the Camp Fire Girls*, 1914, stated:

> The candidate shall further indicate her love and understanding of the Camp Fire ideal by learning ... THE FIRE MAKER'S DESIRE
> As fuel is brought to the fire
> So I purpose to bring
> My strength
> My ambition
> My heart's desire
> My joy
> And my sorrow
> To the fire of humankind.
> For I will tend
> As my fathers have tended
> And my father's fathers
> Since time began
> The fire that is called
> The love of man for man
> The love of man for God.

Y.M.C.A.'S JAMES NAISMITH INVENTED BASKETBALL

James Naismith, a young Y.M.C.A. instructor, was asked by Dr. Luther Gulick, Jr., to devise a game which could be played indoors during the cold winter. This was the origin of basketball.

Naismith was born in 1861 in Ontario, Canada. Both of his parents died of typhoid fever in 1870, when he was just nine years old. He was taken in by his grandmother who died in 1872, leaving him with his Uncle Peter, who stressed self-reliance and reliability.

James worked farm chores, chopped trees, sawed logs, and drove horses. He walked five miles to and from a small school. Though he struggled academically, he learned honesty, initiative, independence, and ruggedness.

A poor student, he left school at age 15 and worked as a lumberjack. It was then that he had a life-changing encounter with Jesus.

Edwin Brit Wyckoff recorded in *The Man who Invented Basketball: James Naismith and His Amazing Game* (Enslow Publishers, Inc, Berkeley Heights, NJ, 2008), the words of James Naismith:

> It was with a firm determination and a great sense of confidence that I was to enter the study for the ministry ... For several years I had been wondering what I wanted to accomplish. Finally I decided that the only real satisfaction that I would ever derive from life was to help my fellow beings.

Naismith added:

> I was lying on the bed on Sunday and thought, "What is this all about? What is life about? What are you going to do? What are you going to be? What motto will you hold up before you?"
>
> I put up on the wall, not in writing, but in my mind this thought: "I want to leave the world a little bit better than I found it."
>
> This is the motto I had then and it is the motto I have today.

With the goal of becoming a minister, he entered McGill University in 1883, located in Montreal, Quebec, Canada. There he studied Philosophy and Hebrew. McGill included athletics as part of the college life. It was there that students organized the very first hockey club in 1877, and wrote the first hockey rule book.

Naismith graduated in 1887, and enrolled to study theology at a McGill–affiliated school, Presbyterian College. To pay his tuition, he worked at McGill as an instructor in physical education.

At Presbyterian College, he was involved in religious activities, the Missionary Society, the Literary and Philosophical Society, and was a staff member of the *Presbyterian College Journal*. He was an avid athlete.

In addition to gymnastics, he played baseball, field hockey, football, rugby and lacrosse – sometimes referred to as "legalized murder."

Dr. Ed and Janice Hird wrote in "Dr. James Naismith: An Examination of the Global Impact of the Basketball Founder" (*Engage Magazine*, 7/2121, engage.lightmagazine.ca) how contact sports resulted in injuries. In playing a game of football, Naismith was kicked in the face and suffered a concussion with temporary memory loss and permanently swollen cauliflower ears.

In response, he and his future wife, Maude Sherman, designed one of football's earliest helmets.

He was advised to leave the evils of the athletic life and devote himself solely to studying and Christian duties. One incident, though, changed his direction.

Naismith liked to play rugby, a game invented at Thomas Arnold's Rugby School in England. During a rugby game in his senior year in seminary, a teammate uttered a profanity. When he looked up and saw James, he embarrassingly apologized and said "I forgot you were there."

James realize that by combining athletics and religious ministry, sports could be used to help men build godly Christian character.

At the age of 29, he came to the United States to work as the physical education teacher at the Young Men's Christian Association department of the School for Christian Workers in Springfield, Massachusetts, renamed the Y.M.C.A. International Training School.

During the harsh New England winter of 1891, the class of young men were bored with calisthenics, sit ups and marching, so Naismith was asked by Dr. Luther Gulick, Jr., to devise a game which could be played indoors.

Alluding to Book of Ecclesiastes, Dr. Gulick told Naismith:

> There is nothing new under the sun. All so-called new things are simply recombinations of the factors of things that are now in existence.

James took the initiative, saying:

> All that we have to do is to take the factors of our known games and then recombine them, and we will have the new game we are looking for.

He also wanted a game that would result in fewer concussions and more sportsmanship.

On December 21, 1891, drawing upon a game he played as a boy, "Duck on a Rock," he created a game of lopping a soccer ball into peach basket.

In a New York radio interview, Naismith said:

> Something had to be done. One day I had an idea. I called the boys to the gym and divided them into two teams of nine and gave them an old soccer ball.
>
> I showed them two peach baskets I had nailed at each end of the gym, and I told them the idea was to throw the ball into the other team's peach basket.

Without rules, brawls would break out on the floor, so Naismith wrote the original 13 rules of basketball, which incorporated aspects of soccer, football and hockey.

With the players not running with the ball, there would be no injuring from tackling as in rugby or football. With the basket up high, there would be less harm near the goal as in hockey.

Professor Michael Zogry, of the University of Kansas Department of Religious Studies, stated:

> Naismith believed an umpire was essential in basketball ... He said an umpire could enforce the rules and remind players how to behave ...
>
> Naismith's hand-written original 13 rules of basketball sold for $4.3 million in 2010. A KU alumnus, David Booth and his wife, Suzanne, purchased the rules as a gift to KU.

In 1899, Naismith's 13 rules were adapted by Senda Berenson Abbott, a Jewish-Lithuanian gymnast instructor at Smith College in

Northampton, Massachusetts, to create a women's version of basketball. She published *Basketball Guide for Women,* 1901–1907, resulting in her being called the "Mother of Women's Basketball."

Dr. Luther Gulick helped Naismith promote basketball. He chaired the Amateur Athletic Union's Basketball Committee, 1895–1905, and was inducted into Basketball's Hall of Fame in 1959. Gulick insisted basketball players abide by high standards of behavior, writing in 1897:

> The game must be kept clean. It is a perfect outrage for an institution that stands for Christian work in the community to tolerate not merely ungentlemanly treatment of guests, but slugging and that which violates the elementary principles of morals ...
> Excuse for the rest of the year, any player who is not clean in his play.

Around this time, another game was developed. Since rugby was causing so many injuries, Yale graduate Walter Camp developed rugby into the safer game called "football" in 1880.

Whereas in rugby players bunched together in a scrummage or "scrum" to move the ball down the field, Camp decided football should have a line of "scrimmage" that moved in plays. Camp is known as the "Father of American Football."

Contributing to the development of football was Coach Amos Alonzo Stagg, a Yale divinity school graduate. Stagg invented the huddle, the center snap, the forward pass, the quarterback keeper, the onside kick, the linebacker position, hip pads, padded goalposts, tackling dummies, and many plays. Stagg was nicknamed "Grand Old Man of Football."

Adding the forward pass to football was John Heisman, who began his coaching career at Oberlin College. The Heisman Trophy is given each year to the most outstanding collegiate football player, such as Tim Tebow in 2007.

Coach "Pop" Warner added headgear, the numbering of players, the three point stance, the spiral punt and, at Carlisle Indian School, he coached Jim Thorpe.

Coach Frank Hering of Notre Dame was one of the first, along with Anna Jarvis, to call for the establishment of a national Mother's Day.

Coach Fielding Yost was on the University of Kansas staff with James Naismith. A devout Christian, he was one of the first coaches to have Jewish players.

Amos Alonzo Stagg joined Naismith at the International Y.M.C.A. Training School as football coach. While there, he recommended basketball be played with only five players on a side. For this contributions, Stagg was inducted into the Basketball Hall of Fame.

In 1924, Stagg coached the U.S. Track and Field Team at the Summer Olympics in Paris, and then coached football at the University of Chicago.

In the football movie, *Knute Rockne, All American,* 1940, starring Ronald Reagan, Stagg appeared in the film, playing the role of himself.

Known for merging sports and religious faith, Stagg stated:

> "I pray not for victory, but to do my best."

> "Winning isn't worthwhile unless one has something finer and nobler behind it. When I reach the soul of one of my boys with an idea, or ideal, or vision, then I have done my job as a coach."
>
> "To me, the coaching profession is one of the noblest and most far-reaching in building manhood."
>
> "No man is too good to be the athletic coach for youth."

James Naismith believed good coaching would produce: "initiative, agility, accuracy, alertness, cooperation, skill, reflex judgment, speed, self-confidence, self-sacrifice, self-control, and sportsmanship." He advocated for racial equality and opposed segregation in all its forms.

KU Professor Michael Zogry, further explained Naismith's approach to sports and faith:

> His approach was to put Christianity out there in front of people and try to influence them through positive character development, but he reserved his formal preaching for when he was a guest minister at area churches.
>
> For Naismith, basketball was not simply a game, but an evangelization tool. Basketball became so popular, that two years later, in 1893, the Y.M.C.A. began promoting it internationally.

Zogry described how Y.M.C.A. missionaries took the game of Basketball around the world.

> Y.M.C.A.s began to integrate the game

into their mission trips and it is recorded that many young people were brought to Christ through these missionaries and the game of basketball.

Y.M.C.A. missionaries first took the game to Canada, then overseas to Japan, the Philippines, Puerto Rico, Cuba, and around the globe. Christian missionaries brought basketball to China through the Y.M.C.A., it has become one of the nation's most popular sports. Y.M.C.A. missionary T.D. Patton took basketball to India.

Another Y.M.C.A. director who created a sport was Juan Carlos Ceriani, a 1936 graduate of the International Y.M.C.A. Training Center. He became Director of the Children's Department at the Y.M.C.A in Montevideo, Uruguay, where in the late 1930s he created the sport of "futsal."

The website futsalfeed.com states of Ceriani:

> He created a new sport, relying heavily on the rules of basketball and other games for inspiration. Over a few years, he developed a heavier ball that was suited to the hard indoor surface.

In bad weather, it was played indoors, five on a side. It became instantly popular in Brazil and spread to the rest of South America, and then Europe. Futsal is now played by millions and is included in the Olympics.

Marshfield, Wisconsin, Y.M.C.A. website (accessed 8/4/25, https://mfldymca.org/about_us/history_national.php) described another sport invented in 1887, a simpler version of baseball, referred to as kittenball or sissyball.

In 1926, Denver Y.M.C.A. member Walter Hakanson proposed the name "softball" and it was adopted. Colorado Y.M.C.A. secretary Homer Hoisington helped standardized the rules. In 1933, the Denver Y.M.C.A. team represented Colorado at the first national softball competition in Chicago.

In 1906, at the Detroit Y.M.C.A., George Corsan developed group swim lessons. In 1910, the Kansas City Y.M.C.A. installed one of the earliest pool filtration systems.

In 1913, at the Y.M.C.A. Training Center in Springfield, George Goss wrote the first book on lifesaving in America. William Ball, a Y.M.C.A. board member, recommended the Red Cross teach lifesaving.

By 1932, a million persons a year were taught to swim at Y.M.C.A.s across America.

In 1949 Joseph G. Sobek, a Y.M.C.A. volunteer in Greenwich, Connecticut invented the sport of racquetball as an alternative to handball, writing the official rules in 1951.

In 1894, James Naismith married Maude, and together they had five children. The next year they moved to Colorado, where James took the position as Physical Education director at the Denver Y.M.C.A.

When his brother, Robbie, died from an infection, James decided to be a doctor. In 1898, he obtained a medical degree from Gross Medical College, which merged in 1912 with the University of Colorado Medical School. Naismith earned four doctorate degrees before age 35.

As a minister, coach and medical doctor,

Naismith was a holistic missionary caring for the whole person — spirit, mind, and body. Moving to Lawrence, Kansas, he was assistant gymnasium director, campus chaplain, and basketball coach for the University of Kansas Jayhawks.

Professor Michael Zogry stated:

> Naismith arrived at KU in 1898 after he had earned a medical degree while employed by the Denver Y.M.C.A.
>
> KU hired him to be the chapel director (daily prayer services were compulsory for students then), campus physician, physical education program director and, yes, the basketball coach ...
>
> In addition to basketball and physical fitness, Naismith nurtured the study of religion at KU.
>
> In 1921, he was among those founding the Kansas School of Religion just a few steps off the university campus. The Kansas School of Religion was a forerunner of KU's Department of Religious Studies.

Zogry wrote of another famous KU coach:

> Forrest Clare (Phog) Allen was not only known as the father of basketball coaching but is thought to have been Naismith's student at KU.

Basketball continued to grow in popularity, being demonstrated at the 1904 Summer Olympics in St. Louis, Missouri.

Dr. Ed and Janice Hird wrote in *Dr. James Naismith: An Examination of the Global Impact of the Basketball Founder* that his sister, Annie, was disappointed that James chose sports ministry instead of being the pastor of a congregation.

Naismith wrote:

> A few years ago, on a visit to my only sister I asked her if she had ever forgiven me for leaving the ministry.
>
> She looked seriously at me, shook here head, and said, "No Jim, you put your hand to the plow and then turned back."
>
> As long as she lived, she never witnessed a basketball game, and I believe that she was a little ashamed to think that I had been the originator of the game.

Naismith saw sports as a platform to build Christian character, instill good sportsmanship, to love your neighbor, to play by the Golden Rule.

He said that he:

> ... could best serve God by influencing young men's characters, being convinced that he could better exemplify the Christian life through sports than in the pulpit.

Naismith wrote:

> Self-control, the subordination of one's feelings for a purpose. The player who permits his feelings to interfere with his reflexes is not only a hindrance to his team, but he is also occupying a place that might better be filled by another.

Naismith believed sports provided an opportunity to develop strength to stand in faith to fight life's battles, strength to live a fulfilled live in accordance with the Bible, and strength to serve others, developing:

> ... a willingness to place the good of the team above one's personal ambitions ... playing the game vigorously, observing the rules definitely, accepting defeat gracefully, and winning courteously.

He added:

> I may say in conclusion: Let us all be able to lose gracefully and to win courteously; to accept criticism as well as praise; and last of all, to appreciate the attitude of the other fellow at all times.

Naismith explained:

> There is no place in basketball for the egotist.

In 1911, Naismith published the book, *A Modern College*. When World War I started in 1914, he volunteered at the age of 54.

Though he was Canadian, he was able to get official ordination credentials from the Presbyterian Church and be appointed by the governor as an honorary captain and chaplain of the nascent First Kansas Infantry.

In 1916, he was stationed at Fort Riley, Kansas, where two years later the Spanish Flu broke out. His unit was transferred to Eagle Pass, Texas, where soldiers served as guards during the Mexican Border War with Pancho Villa.

James Patton wrote in "Remembering a Veteran: Dr. James Naismith, Y.M.C.A." (Roads to the Great War, April 2, 2018):

> Naismith took his calling as chaplain very seriously, approaching it like coaching a team of his young players, encouraging them to realize

their potential. He conducted church services, counseled soldiers, and advised commanding officers as to the spiritual needs of the unit.

His concern was to keep troops from gambling, alcohol, brawls and prostitutes. He kept them busy being physically fit, organizing basketball games, baseball games, and boxing matches involving the entire garrison at Eagle Pass.

James Patton described Naismith's emphasis on Biblical morality:

> In June 1917 Naismith was accepted as a lecturer on "moral conditions and sex education." His job was training counselors, inspiring troops and developing programs to improve morale and morality.
>
> His experience in this work formed a large part of the material for his book, *Essence of a Healthy Life*, 1918.
>
> In the fall of 1918, he was sent to France as a Y.M.C.A. Overseas Secretary, where his work continued as before but now in the shadow of the front. He wrote ... "I feel that I'm fitted for this work." With his breadth of experience, probably no one was a better choice.

James Patton recorded a statement Naismith wrote while in France:

> It is a pretty big job ... go over and make the camps clean places for the boys to fight. And also get the right spirit into the men. That involves two things.
>
> Educate the men and eliminate

> the evils from the camps and vicinity. Pershing is very anxious to have this done. I go without instructions to find out the best thing to do and then get the machinery working. It is no child's play, especially when it is among the old-fashioned type of soldier and in France where ideals are so different.
>
> The responsibility is great but I am going into it determined. I do wish that you and the family would pray for me, for I have never felt so much in need of help as I do at this present minute.

Of his 19 months with the Y.M.C.A. in France, Naismith said he was thankful for:

> ... the knowledge that I have tried to help the people of the world to make it a little better, and that I have tried to love my neighbor as myself.

Returning stateside as a 57-year-old war veteran, he resumed his position as director of physical education at the University of Kansas. In 1925, he officially became an American citizen.

Three years before his death, he saw basketball recognized as an official event at the 1936 Summer Olympic Games in Berlin. Though he shunned publicity, he agreed to throw the jump ball at the opening ceremony. After the games, he was chosen to hand out the medals: U.S.A. won gold; Canada won silver; and Mexico won bronze.

In 1937, he helped form what became the National Association of Intercollegiate Athletics–NAIA.

In 1939, just eight months after the birth of the National Collegiate Athletic Association–NCAA

Basketball Championships, Dr. James Naismith died at the age of 78. He challenged the NCAA to:

> Use every means to put basketball (as) a factor in the molding of character.

One of his players remembered:

> With him, questions of physical development inevitably led to questions of moral development, and vice versa.

The Journal of Health and Physical Education praised Naismith as "a physician who encouraged healthful living through participation through vigorous activities" building "character in the hearts of young men."

Basketball grew to be one of the biggest sports in North America, with 24 million participating in 2009 according to the U.S. Census Bureau, and played by over 450 million worldwide. Only soccer is more popular.

In 2015 "March Madness" attracted 80.7 million people worldwide who watched the tournament online.

Unlike athletes today, Naismith did not profit from inventing basketball. He even lost two houses to foreclosure Jayson Jenks wrote in "The Rules of the Game: Bill Self, Kansas, and Basketball History," March 22, 2012:

> Naismith never cashed in on his creation. He had offers to do commercials and advertisement campaigns, but except for lending his name as endorsement for a Rawlings basketball, he declined.
>
> Naismith stayed committed to his mission, which was ... to win men for

the Master (Jesus) through the gym.

Naismith stated:

> I am sure that no man can derive more satisfaction from money or power than I do from seeing a pair of basketball goals in some out of the way place. Deep in the Wisconsin woods ... High in the Colorado mountains ... halfway across the desert ... all are constant reminders that I have at least partially accomplished the objective that I set up.

Basketball nets adorn garages, walls, barns, schools and Y.M.C.A.s in communities across the globe. It was the first game requiring gymnasium's to have high ceilings. Naismith wrote:

> Whenever I witness games in a church league, I feel that my vision, almost half a century ago, of the time when the Christian people would recognize the true value of athletics, has become a reality.

Two years after his death, Naismith's book, *Basketball—its Origins and Development*, was published in 1941. Jon Ackerman wrote in the article "Upward Sports is carrying out the vision of the late Dr. James Naismith" (*Sports Spectrum Magazine*, Winter 2017):

> Dr. James Naismith invented basketball as a way to reach young people for Jesus. That same vision is fueling Upward Sports, the world's largest Christian youth sports organization ...
>
> James Pomeroy Naismith, now 81, is the last living grandson of Dr. Naismith. He was 3 when his famous grandfather

passed away ...

Speaking of his grandfather, "He could see a potential for an outreach, a Christian outreach to young people using competitive sports, and it is perfectly clear that he himself loved competitive sports ...

If you can take something you love and apply it not only to your life, but through outreach to give others a better life, now that's a really good vision."

Naismith is honored in eight Canadian and American Halls of Fame, and is featured on both Canadian and the United States postage stamps.

KU Professor Michael Zogry stated:

Naismith's goals in life, as he stated on his application to the International Y.M.C.A. Training School, were to try to help "win men for the Master," to build character and to be an example for the men.

Zogry added:

The story of Naismith's creation of the game is widely known ... Less well-known is that his game also was meant to help build Christian character and to inculcate certain values of the muscular Christian movement.

Edwin Brit Wyckoff described how both James Naismith and Theodore Roosevelt admired British author Thomas Hughes' popular book, *Tom Brown's Schooldays*, 1857:

Muscular Christianity is Christianity applied to the treatment and use of our bodies. It is an enforcement of the laws of health by the solemn sanctions of the New Testament.

❧

Y.M.C.A.'S WILLIAM MORGAN INVENTED VOLLEYBALL

In 1892, a student of Dr. Luther Gulick's at the International Y.M.C.A. Training School in Springfield, Massachusetts, was William Morgan, who had been recruited there by James Naismith after he had seen him play football.

After graduating, Morgan became physical education director at the Y.M.C.A. in Holyoke, Massachusetts. It was there that Morgan invented the game of Volleyball in 1895.

Morgan wrote the original rules for volleyball and printed them in the first edition of the *Official Handbook of the Athletic League of the Young Men's Christian Associations of North America* (1897). To avoid injuries, he asked A.G. Spalding & Brothers of Chicopee, Massachusetts, to design a ball that was lighter than a basketball.

Volleyball quickly spread across America and to other countries. In 1916, the Y.M.C.A. volleyball rules were shared with the NCAA — National Collegiate Athletic Association.

The first official volleyball tournament was held by the National Y.M.C.A. Physical Education Committee in New York City in 1922.

In 1928, the U.S. Volleyball Association was formed and began to organize tournaments nationwide. As of 2009, the U.S. Census Bureau statistics (2009) reported over 10 million Americans play volleyball.

Rev. Dr. Ed & Janice Hird wrote "William G. Morgan, missionary inventor of Volleyball," September 15, 2022, which gave some background:

Few people know that two of the most popular sports, basketball and volleyball, were both invented by Christian missionaries in the 1890s as evangelistic sports.

Who might have imagined that 127 years later, over 46 million North Americans and 800 million people globally would now participate in volleyball?

Born in 1870 at Lockport, New York, William G. Morgan loved working at his father's boat yard on the banks of the Old Erie Canal.

Like many young men, he wanted to be just like his dad. So, at age 14, he initially ran away from home to work on a canal boat.

At age 15, William dropped out of school because he felt awkward about being larger than most of his classmates. His godly mother, seeing his academic gifting, had him apply to the famous evangelist Dwight L. Moody's Mount Hermon School for Boys.

A local pastor, R. Norton, supported Will's application, stating,

> He is very thoughtful and interested in spiritual things. He is very reliable and has much symmetry of character.

Morgan's Sunday School teacher wrote this endorsement of the Morgan family:

> His mother is a remarkable woman. A devout Christian, a "main stay" in her Church; calm, quiet, dignified in her bearing, she purchases ably and shows great executive ability earnestly and most devoutly does she work and pray for the good of young people of East Lockport. Respectfully, L.F. Helmer (Mrs. J.S.)

Morgan's initial application was not accepted. Fortunately, his persistent Sunday School teacher sent a second endorsement letter, saying,

> I simply write to ask attention to it, as his call is critical. If Will is not accepted now, for term beginning in February, there is great reason to fear he will never go to school again. Not from his wish, but from circumstances ... A thoroughly established Christian, inheriting from his mother superior qualities of mind and heart, he is well worth polishing for his Master's use.
> I beg your attention to his application. Respectfully, Mrs. J.S. Helmer.

Within a week, Morgan was accepted into Mount Hermon School for Boys, where he studied Bible, academics, music, and sports. While singing on evangelistic tours, he fell in love with the pianist, Mary King Caldwell, his future wife.

Football became his passion. When the Mount Hermon football team held its own against the superstar Y.M.C.A. Springfield team, Morgan was recruited four days later by the Springfield Coach Dr. James Naismith.

Springfield College was part of the muscular

Christianity movement, creating such a strong football team that they defeated the best of the University teams, Harvard, Yale, and Princeton.

After Naismith received a nasty concussion, he wanted a kinder, more Christian sport, basketball.

Morgan, who was mentored by Naismith, became the Y.M.C.A. physical education director in Holyoke, Massachusetts. There, he noticed that basketball was too rigorous for middle-aged people. So, in 1895, he invented volleyball, as a gentler spin-off from basketball.

As a non-contact sport, there were far fewer bloody noses. In creating volleyball, Morgan adapted ideas from handball, baseball, tennis, and badminton. His desire was to invent a new game which everyone could play, regardless of their age or physical ability.

Initially he called it "mintonette." At the suggestion of Y.M.C.A. Training Center Professor Alfred Halstead, he renamed it "volleyball."

Needing a lighter ball than a basketball, he asked A.G. Spalding to create one. Writing the original rules for volleyball, Morgan printed them in the first edition of the *Official Handbook of the Athletic League of the Young Men's Christian Associations of North America* (1897).

In 1900, Canada became the first country outside of the USA to adopt the game. Y.M.C.A. missionaries quickly introduced Volleyball to missionary schools in Asia. It was so popular, it was played in the Oriental Games in 1913.

Once again, it was Y.M.C.A. missionaries who ministered to the body, mind and spirit through volleyball: Hyozo Omori and Franklin Brown in Japan (1908), Elwood S. Brown in the Philippines (1910), J. Howard Crocker in China, and Dr. J.H. Gray in Burma, China & India.

Volleyball, like basketball, was truly a missionary sport with global impact.

In the early Y.M.C.A., founded by the evangelist Sir George Williams, they didn't just play sports. Before each game, they would have a time of Christ-centered bible study and prayer with the sports team.

Volleyball caught on in Russia through the Y.M.C.A. When the Y.M.C.A.s were kicked out of socialist Russia in 1927 for being religious, volleyball was allowed to stay. Russia's teams became dominant globally. During WWI, American troops brought volleyball to Europe.

Volleyball was first demonstrated in the 1924 Paris Olympics, but not added as an official Olympic sport until 1964. Beach volleyball did not get accepted in the Olympics until 1996.

Rev. Dr. Ed & Janice Hird ended their historical review, "William G. Morgan, missionary inventor of Volleyball," with a credit:

> We thank God for William G. Morgan, an amazingly creative missionary, who left us with a healthy, non-violent sport that has impacted the world.

Y.M.C.A. CHAPTERS AROUND THE WORLD

Soon after being founded, Y.M.C.A. chapters opened around the world. Wikipedia's entry for "Y.M.C.A." (accessed 1/24/25) has:

> From its inception, the Y.M.C.A. grew rapidly, ultimately becoming a worldwide movement founded on the principles of muscular Christianity ... a para-church organization based on Protestant values.

The Y.M.C.A. is the oldest and largest youth organization in the world, reaching 65 million people with 90,000 staff and 920,000 volunteers, in chapters located in 120 countries, grouped into seven regions: Africa, Asia and the Pacific, Europe, Latin America and the Caribbean, Canada, USA, and the Middle East.

Some of the oldest chapters are: Australia, 1851; the United States, 1851; Italy, 1851; France, 1852; Switzerland, 1852; New Zealand, 1855; Jamaica, 1857; South Africa, 1865; Pakistan, 1876; Japan, 1880; Spain, 1880; Barbados, 1880; Sri Lanka, 1882; Germany, 1883; Mexico, 1891; Greece, 1892; Brazil, 1893; China, 1895; India, 1895; Myanmar, 1897; Philippines, 1898; Russia, 1900; Hong Kong, 1901; Argentina, 1902; Korea, 1903; Malaysia, 1905; Uruguay, 1909; Egypt, 1909; Chile, 1912; Turkey, 1914; Romania, 1919; Peru, 1920; Trinidad and Tobago, 1921; Indonesia, 1928; Singapore, 1941; Taiwan, 1945; Uganda, 1959; Ecuador, 1959.

In India, a Y.M.C.A. was opened in Calcutta in 1854, in Bombay in 1875, and Madras in 1890.

Dr. J. Henry Gray, a 1904 graduate from the International Y.M.C.A. Training School in Springfield, Massachusetts, became director of the Y.M.C.A. Physical Education Program in India, 1908, being the first trained physical director from the West.

He was so successful that the government of India recommended Dr. Gray's methods be standardized throughout the empire and he became an advisor to the government.

In 1911, Y.M.C.A. chapters in India held their first physical training course in Calcutta.

In 1912, they moved it to Bangalore near Union Theological College of South India and Ceylon, a school co-sponsored by the London Missionary Society, the Wesleyan Methodist Missionary Society, The United Free Church of Scotland, the Arcot Mission of the Dutch Reformed Church in America.

By 1913, India's National Council of Y.M.C.A.s established in Madras the Department of Physical Education and organized a national athletic meet, but it had to be postponed due to World War I.

In 1920, Harry Crowe Buck, a graduate of the International Y.M.C.A. Training School in Springfield, Massachusetts, established the first College of Physical Education in Madras, working with India's National Council of Y.M.C.A.s.

Buck organized courses in physical education, anatomy, physiology, hygiene, tropical hygiene, sanitation, first aid, and playgrounds. The college had additional courses in Bible study, administration, English composition, physical exercise, and the Boy Scouts.

Harry Buck's wife, Marie, taught physical education to Indian women, publishing *A Programme of Physical Education for Girls' Schools in India.* The College of Physical Education in Madras grew from 5 students to 500.

Sir John Ernest Hodder-Williams, nephew of George Williams, wrote in the book, *The Father of the Red Triangle, The Life of Sir George Williams, Founder of the Y.M.C.A.*, 1918:

> What would George Williams, the founder, and to the end of his long life the very heart and soul of the Young Men's Christian Association, have thought of the way in which his work has been enlarged on every side, of the manner in which it has entered into every phase of usefulness for young men?
>
> However elaborate and many-sided the work of the Y.M.C.A. may be or may become, it is built on the broad and firm foundation he laid and his ambitions for his Master's work knew no bounds of time or space.
>
> Throughout his life he preached unceasingly the power of individual work for individual men, the supreme importance of bringing religion into most intimate personal touch with the daily conflict ...
>
> If you will read of how George Williams, from his early days, looked out upon the world as a general surveying a crowded battleground, as one before whom, very really and literally, the forces

of good and evil, of Christ and Satan, were daily and hourly engaged in deadly battle, you will understand how naturally the Association he founded adapted itself to meet the needs of the days of war.

JACK BOYD, Y.M.C.A. DIRECTOR

Worldwide Y.M.C.A. chapters had a focus on spreading Christianity on a day-to-day basis.

Jack E. Boyd was director of the Y.M.C.A. at the University of Oklahoma. In 1892, he published a pamphlet, "WHY THE "Y", which gives insight into day-to-day operations of Y.M.C.A. chapters:

> WHAT IS THE Y.M.C.A.
>
> The Young Men's Christian Association of the University of Oklahoma is the organized result of a student movement to unite the spiritual and moral forces of the campus for the purpose of developing and conserving Christian manhood.
>
> It is an association of men students who are seeking to apply the morality of Jesus Christ to the concrete every day experience of university life.
>
> WHO ARE ITS MEMBERS
>
> Any student or faculty man desiring to identify himself with the objective of the Y.M.C.A. may become a member. There are no membership dues. Membership is given on the basis of interest and service. Every member has voting privileges.

WHO RUNS IT

The Y.M.C.A. is a democratic organization. The membership has final authority through the ballot box. Officers are elected for a one year term.

The president with other elected officials choose a cabinet of 10 or 12 men who become responsible for the Association program.

These men are assisted in their work by committees. Any one desiring a place on this promotion force need merely to indicate the work he wishes to do.

The Advisory Board consists of 11 men from the faculty and men of the community elected to the cabinet have oversight of the business affairs of the Association and employ the General Secretary.

WHAT ARE ITS PURPOSES

The Y.M.C.A. of the University of Oklahoma is a union of students and faculty members of the University formed for the following purposes:

1. To lead students to faith in God through Jesus Christ.

2. To lead them into membership and service in the Christian church.

3. To promote their growth in Christian faith, especially through study of the Bible and prayer.

4. To influence them to devote themselves in a united effort with all Christians to making the will of Christ effective in all human society and to extending the Kingdom of God throughout the world.

WHAT IS ITS PROGRAM

The Y.M.C.A.'s program is not a series of isolated events or stunts. The building is not the Y.M.C.A. but it is only the headquarters; the program is on the campus and in the lives of men.

WHAT IS ITS CONNECTION WITH THE CHURCHES

The Y.M.C.A. is an interdenominational organization. One of its purposes as stated in the constitution is "to lead students into membership and service in the Christian church." It represents the united churches on the campus and its mission is to supplement and strengthen the work of the churches.

HOW IS IT FINANCED

There are no membership dues. Membership means conviction, not money. Expenses of promoting its program are provided by voluntary contributions. The individual member must determine the extent of his support to the association.

WHY JOIN THE "Y"

Because you endorse its purpose and program. Because you believe in it. Because you want to help it. Because it is your organization. Because of the good it can do. Because of the help that participation in its programs will do for you.

Sign the application card. Become a member. Boost the organization. Make the "Y" a vital force in your life and on the Sooner campus.

Jack Boyd's pamphlet revealed how the Y.M.C.A. activities have been adopted as a normal part of campus life, such as student housing, freshman orientation, job placement, social mixers, clubs, athletic competitions, talent shows, sandwich and coffee shops.

ACTIVITIES

Rooms: A list of rooms is kept on file at the Y.M.C.A. office and serves the men at the beginning of the year.

Employment: Hundreds of men are assisted in getting permanent jobs through the employment office. Odd jobs are handled during the entire year. The amount runs into the thousands of dollars.

Freshman Handbook: Three thousand handbooks are distributed to University students with special emphasis on freshmen. This assists them in getting acquainted with the University and its traditions.

Social Affairs: A freshman dinner, stage mixer and numerous joint social affairs with the Y.W.C.A. are given each year in order that the student body may get better acquainted.

Special Meetings: Each year a number of speakers of national prominence are brought to the campus. An evangelistic campaign is conducted each year by a man who knows student religious problems.

Church Attendance: Through the system of having representatives from all denominations on the cabinet, assistance is given to the churches in reaching their membership. Affiliation Day comes early in the year when students are urged to affiliate with their church.

Community Service: Churches are

conducted in four nearby communities where there is no regular pastor and numerous teams sent to nearby high schools to carry the message of clean living to high school boys.

Boys Work: Hi-Y Clubs are fostered in Norman and University high schools. Last year these were the strongest in the state.

Student Forum: A student forum handling the fundamentals of Christian thinking is held during the fall semester. This gives men the opportunity to shape their religious faith.

Student Conferences: This had grown to be a tradition in Soonerland. On this night the best vaudeville talent in the University preforms for the student body.

Building: The building includes offices for the Association, the Student Council, and the Student Union. In addition there is a reading room and a Waffle and Sandwich Shop. In the Waffle Shop food is served to students at a minimum cost. Approximately five thousand meals are served each month. It is not run for profit.

Track Meet: The Association has the responsibility for placing the thousands of men who come each year for the track meet. This is done without charge.

(Special thanks to Jack Boyd's relative Bennetta Lou Yaeger of Broken Arrow, Oklahoma, for preserving the above pamphlet.)

Y.M.C.A. LED IN RACIAL RECONCILIATION

Jack Boyd became director of the Denver Y.M.C.A. He corresponded with the famous black scientist Dr. George Washington Carver.

On March 1, 1927, Carver wrote to Jack Boyd:

> My beloved friend, keep your hand in that of the Master, walk daily by His side, so that you may lead others into the realms of true happiness, where a religion of hate, (which poisons both body and soul) will be unknown, having in its place the "Golden Rule" way, which is the "Jesus Way" of life, will reign supreme ...
>
> Then, we can walk and talk with Jesus momentarily, because we will be attuned to His will and wishes, thus making the Creation story of the world nondebatable as to its reality.

The Young Men's Christian Association was at the forefront of racial reconciliation and desegregation. In 1915, at Chicago's Wabash Avenue Y.M.C.A., Carter Woodson organized the "Association for the Study of Negro Life and History." This grew into Negro History Week, which became Black History Month, officially declared by President Gerald Ford in 1976.

In 1920, the Paseo Y.M.C.A. in Kansas City, organized the Negro National League, the first black baseball league to last a full season.

In 1947, Jackie Robinson broke the color barrier and became the first Black major league baseball player in 1947. He was a volunteer boys coach at the Harlem Y.M.C.A. with fellow coach and teammate Roy Campanella.

The Y.M.C.A. promoted *A Pictorial History of the Negro in America* by Langston Hughes and Milton Meltzer, 1956.

A leader in racial healing was the founder of Blue Ridge Assembly Y.M.C.A. in North Carolina, Dr. Willis D. Weatherford, who stated:

> Blue Ridge has probably done more than any other single institution to make the white people of the South conscious of their responsibility to serve this largest minority group in America ...
>
> The spirit of cooperation developed there has sent thousands of the choicest college students back to their respective colleges or out into the world as advocates of better racial understanding.

He added:

> It is not the negro that is on trial before the world, but it is we, the white men of the South.

Dr. Weatherford courageously invited Tuskegee professor George Washington Carver to speak. After the introduction, Dr. Carver humorously exclaimed:

> I always look forward to introductions as opportunities to learn something about myself ...

Carver gave God credit for his inspiration:

> Years ago, I went into my laboratory and said, "Dear Mr. Creator, please tell me what

the universe was made for?"

The Great Creator answered, "You want to know too much for that little mind of yours. Ask for something more your size, little man."

Then I asked, "Please, Mr. Creator, tell me what man was made for."

Again, the Great Creator replied, "You are still asking too much. Cut down on the extent and improve the intent" ...

So then I asked, "Please, Mr. Creator, will you tell me why the peanut was made?"

"That's better, but even then it's infinite. What do you want to know about the peanut?"

"Mr. Creator, can I make milk out of the peanut?"

"What kind of milk do you want? Good Jersey milk or just plain boarding house milk?"

"Good Jersey milk." And then the

Great Creator taught me to take the peanut apart and put it together again. And out of the process have come forth all these products!

Carver wrote in *A Brief Sketch of My Life*, 1922:

> I would never allow anyone to give me money, no difference how badly I needed it. I wanted literally to earn my living.

Blue Ridge Y.M.C.A. founder Dr. Weatherford taught on the importance of manual labor, writing:

> The experience of slavery had left a deep psychological scar on the South and its attitude toward work ... The slave hated labor because it branded him as inferior, and the white man shunned labor because he thought it was the slave's province ... (but) any task which added richness to

human existence was a sacred task.

When a staff member complained about manual labor, Weatherford responded,

> You had better change your attitude toward both work and Negroes—or leave Blue Ridge. We respect both here.

In 1928, Dr. George Washington Carver wrote:

> Human need is really a great spiritual vacuum which God seeks to fill ... With one hand in the hand of a fellow man in need and the other in the hand of Christ, He could get across the vacuum ... Then the passage, "I can do all things through Christ which strengthens me," came to have real meaning.

On March 24, 1925, Carver wrote to Robert Johnson of Chesley Enterprises of Ontario:

> Thank God I love humanity; complexion doesn't interest me one single bit.

In 1939, he was awarded the Roosevelt Medal, with the declaration:

> To a scientist humbly seeking the guidance of God and a liberator to men of the white race as well as the black.

FIRST FATHER'S DAY

The first annual Father's Day celebration involved the Y.M.C.A. in Spokane, Washington. It began when Sonora Louise Smart Dodd heard a church sermon on the newly established Mother's Day in 1908. She wanted to honor her father, Civil War veteran William Jackson Smart, who had raised six children by himself after his wife died in childbirth.

Sonora drew up a petition supported by the Young Men's Christian Association and the ministers of Spokane to celebrate Father's Day on June 19, 1910. The next year it spread to Oregon, then Chicago, then across the nation.

In 1916, President Wilson sent a telegraph message to the Spokane Father's Day service.

Y.M.C.A. DURING WORLD WAR I

Thousands of Y.M.C.A. members felt it was their duty to immediately volunteer and support the Allied troops during World War I.

The Y.M.C.A. conducted 90 percent of the welfare work among the armed services in Europe during the war, assuming military responsibilities on a scale that had never been attempted by any nonprofit organization in history.

Y.M.C.A. operations included 1,500 canteens and exchanges. It also set up 4,000 huts and tents for religious services and recreation. Volunteers sustained 286 casualties, with 319 being awarded citations for brave service. The Y.M.C.A. engaged in prisoner-of-war efforts, providing supplies and aid to over 5 million prisoners.

Princess Helena Victoria of Schleswig-Holstein created the first Y.M.C.A. Women's Auxiliary during the first month of WWI. When the U.S. entered the war in 1917, there were 5,145 women engaged in Y.M.C.A. war services.

British Y.M.C.A. secretary Arthur Yapp had volunteers wear armbands with Dr. Luther Gulick's red triangle logo, which was also placed on the thousands of Y.M.C.A. huts, tents, tea bars and restrooms run for military personnel. Y.W.C.A. workers wore a similar blue triangle.

Sir John Ernest Hodder-Williams, nephew of George Williams, wrote in the book, *The Father of the Red Triangle, The Life of Sir George Williams, Founder of the Y.M.C.A.*, 1918:

> He builded better than he ever knew or, optimist that he was, ever could dream. This is not the place to attempt to tell of the work of the Y.M.C.A. during the war, of the wonder of that Association which shares with the Red Cross the honor of being the greatest voluntary organization known to history, which shares with it too, the splendid triumph of having exalted Christianity and the Cross before the eyes of a world that had almost lost sight of both in the foul fog of a Prussian-made materialism ...
>
> It is impossible to imagine what would have happened to our soldiers, sailors, and munition makers, to those who are winning the war for us, had there been no Y.M.C.A. to care for and comfort and cheer them.
>
> That statement is a commonplace among the greatest men in all English-speaking land; a universally admitted ...

George Williams spent himself, all he had and was, in marshaling, strengthening, heartening Christian young men that they might overcome the foe; a master of religious strategy and tactics, he realized that every means must be protect his, Christ's, army against the assaults of the enemy and to arm men physically, mentally, morally for the fight — and so it was that the readiness of the Y.M.C.A. to undertake the million cares, to face the unnumbered problems of the world war was not the miraculous inspiration of a moment but just the glorious working out of the plans designed so many years before by the Father of the Red Triangle.

A U.S. Army soldier was composer Irving Berlin, whose Jewish family had immigrated from Russia to America. His father had been an itinerant cantor who sang in synagogues.

As a streetboy in New York, Berlin sold newspapers to help his family. When he sang to get people's attention, some threw coins to him. He told his mother that is when he decided to pursue a singing career.

As a soldier, Irving Berlin was stationed at Fort Yaphank in 1918, inspiring him to wrote a musical review to raise military morale, Yip Yip Yaphank, which included the song "I Can Always Find a Little Sunshine in the Y.M.C.A."

At the same time a song was written by Ed Rose and Abe Olman, The Meaning of Y.M.C.A. (You Must Come Across), with the lyrics:

They've done their bit and more.

> To help us win the war ...
> The Y is right there on the firing line.

In 1917, the Y.M.C.A. produced a pocket-sized New Testament for the Army. It was given to the millions of soldiers heading to France and Belgium. President Wilson wrote the foreword:

> The Bible is the Word of Life. I beg that you will read it and find this out for yourselves, –read, not little snatches here and there, but long passages that will really be the road to the heart of it.
>
> You will find it full of real men and women not only, but also of the things you have wondered about and been troubled about all your life, as men have been always;
>
> – and the more you read the more it will become plain to you what things are worthwhile and what are not, what things make men happy,–loyalty, right dealing, speaking the truth, readiness to give everything for what they think their duty,
>
> – and, most of all, the wish that they may have the approval of the Christ, who gave everything for them, and the things that are guaranteed to make men unhappy,–selfishness, cowardice, greed, and everything that is low and mean.
>
> When you have read the Bible, you will know it is the Word of God, because you will have found in it the key to your own heart, your own happiness, and your own duty. –(signed) Woodrow Wilson.

The Y.M.C.A. also published a New Testament for the National War Work Council in 1918, and a New Testament for the American Navy.

The British Y.M.C.A. distributed New Testaments with a foreword by Field Marshall Lord Roberts, August 25, 1914:

> I ask you to put your trust in God. He will watch over you and strengthen you.
> You will find in this little Book guidance when you are in health, comfort when you are in sickness, and strength when you are in adversity.

The New Testament had a page titled "War Roll" and underneath:

> I hereby pledge my allegiance to the Lord Jesus Christ as my Savior and King, and by God's help will fight His battles for the Victory of His Kingdom.
> Name ....
> Regiment and No. ....
> Home Address ....
> Date ....

On the opposite page is:

> Y.M.C.A. War League "Thy Kingdom Come"
> 1. The War League is founded to league Soldiers together under the Standard of the Cross.
> 2. Its principle is Service of Humanity under Christ.
> 3. Its preparation is Self-Discipline for the welfare of others.
> 4. Its atmosphere is Communion with God.
> 5. Its Orders are found in this Book.
> If willing, sign the opposite page and sign our Roll, send postcard giving Name, Regiment and Number, Home Address and Denomination to Y.M.C.A., Russell Sq.,

London, W.C. You will then be enrolled and a card of membership sent to you.

President Woodrow Wilson addressed the 70th anniversary of the Y.M.C.A., October 24, 1914:

> Christ came into the world to save others, not to save Himself; and no man is a true Christian who does not think constantly of how he can lift his brother.

Wilson continued:

> I do believe that at 70, the Y.M.C.A. is just reaching its majority. A dream greater even than George Williams ever dreamed will be realized in the great accumulating momentum of Christian men throughout the world ...
>
> These 70 years have just been a running start ... now there will be a great rush of Christian principle upon the strongholds of evil and of wrong in the world.
>
> Those strongholds are not as strong as they look ... All you have to do is to fight, not with cannon but with light ... That, in my judgment, is what the Young Men's Christian Association can do ...
>
> Eternal vigilance is the price, not only of liberty, but of a great many other things ... It is the price of one's own soul ... What shall he give in exchange for his own soul, or any other man's soul? ...
>
> There is a text in Scripture ... It says godliness is profitable in this life as well as in the life that is to come ... This world is intended as the place in which we shall show that we know how to grow in the stature of manliness and of righteousness.

I have come here to bid Godspeed to the great work of the Young Men's Christian Association.

After World War I, Chinese laborers were brought to Europe to dig trenches, unload ships, and clear battlefields. Y.M.C.A. secretaries from China assisted them. One Y.M.C.A. worker in France was Yale graduate Y.C. James Yen. He created a Chinese alphabet of 100 characters which helped end illiteracy in China.

Y.M.C.A. Projects during the war were so successful that some were institutionalized, such as recreation; overseas exchanges; educational scholarships; welfare, and R&R for combat-weary soldiers.

After World War I, some viewed Y.M.C.A. staff as professional service providers rather than Christian missionaries. The International Y.M.C.A. Training Center had graduates hired for managerial skills above evangelistic.

When Lawrence Doggett was appointed president, a gradual shift occurred till it separated into Springfield College.

YOUNG MEN'S HEBREW ASSOCIATION

Mosaic Magazine published "From the YMHA to the JCC: The Development of Jewish Communal Centers," January 23, 2019:

With its first branch founded New York City in 1874, the Young Men's Hebrew Association—joined in 1888 by the Young Women's Hebrew Association—soon became an important feature of Jewish communal life ...

Jenna Weissman Joselit explains ...

At first, some American Jews conceived of the Y.M.H.A. as an alternative to the Young Men's Christian Association ... Often the only public place in town with a gymnasium, the Y.M.C.A. attracted a growing number of American Jewish men eager to be physically fit, arousing concerns lest they be led astray ...

Others thought of a Jewish "Y" ... as an opportunity for "developing the manhood of" American Jews, a place where, amid dignified conversation, chess matches, and rounds of calisthenics, they might find "something of their own" ...

It didn't take long, though, before the Y.M.H.A. became mired in controversy ... from rabbis who fretted lest the organization undermine the primacy of the synagogue ...

As Joselit describes, these criticisms led to the creation of alternative Jewish centers that combined synagogue and recreational activities ... the Jewish Community Centers.

RED CROSS DURING WORLD WAR I

President Woodrow Wilson cited the Red Cross in his Contribution Day Proclamation for aid of stricken Jewish people, January 11, 1916:

> Whereas in the various countries now engaged in war, there are nine millions of Jews, the great majority of whom are destitute of food, shelter, and clothing; and ... have been driven from their homes without warning, deprived of an opportunity to make provision for their most elementary wants, causing starvation, disease and untold suffering; and ...
>
> Whereas the people of the United States ... have learned with sorrow of this terrible plight of millions of human beings and have most generously responded to the cry for help ...
>
> Now, Therefore, I ... proclaim January 27, 1916, as a day upon which the people of the United States may make such contributions as they feel disposed for the aid of the stricken Jewish people ...
>
> Contributions may be addressed to the American Red Cross, Washington, D.C., which will care for their proper distribution.

Opening the Second Red Cross Drive in New York City, Wilson stated, May 18, 1918:

> Being members of the American Red Cross ... a great fraternity and fellowship which extends all over the world ... This cross which these ladies bore here today is an emblem of Christianity itself ...

> When you think of this, you realize how the people of the United States are being drawn together into a great intimate family whose heart is being used for the service of the soldiers not only, but for the long night of suffering and terror, in order that they and men everywhere may see the dawn of a day of righteousness and justice and peace.

On December 8, 1918, a month after the fighting in World War I had ceased, Wilson appealed for support of the American Red Cross:

> One year ago, twenty-two million Americans, by enrolling as members of the Red Cross at Christmas time, sent to the men who were fighting our battles overseas, a stimulating message of cheer and good-will ...
> Now, by God's grace, the Red Cross Christmas message of 1918 is to be a message of peace as well as a message of good-will."

EVANGELINE BOOTH AND THE SALVATION ARMY

In 1904, William and Catherine Booth's daughter, Evangeline, became the Commander of The Salvation Army's United States forces.

Under her leadership, they evangelized and organized programs for unwed mothers, the homeless and relief during disasters, especially after the 1906 San Francisco earthquake.

During World War I, they staffed canteens to care for soldiers. Evangeline Booth was awarded the Distinguished Service Medal by President Woodrow Wilson in 1919.

The New York Times published an article on August 7, 1927

> FAR–FLUNG ACTIVITY OF SALVATION ARMY; Wherever One Goes in New York It Is to Be Found "Just Around the Corner." IT HAS 47 INSTITUTIONS These Range Through Training Schools to Hospitals, Nurseries, Refuges and Homes.

Evangeline then became International Commander-in-Chief of the Salvation Army, receiving a telegram from President Franklin D. Roosevelt, September 4, 1934:

> Please accept my sincere congratulations on your election as General of The Salvation Army throughout the world.
>
> In these troubled times it is particularly important that the leadership of all good forces shall work for the amelioration of human suffering and for the preservation of the highest spiritual ideals ...
>
> Your efforts as Commander-in-Chief of The Salvation Army ... have earned the gratitude and admiration of millions of your countrymen.

REV. EDGAR HELMS FOUNDED GOODWILL INDUSTRIES

A Christian inspired to meet a need was United Methodist minister Rev. Edgar James Helms who founded Goodwill Industries in 1902

The Goodwill website (accessed 1/17/25) posts the biography of Edgar James Helms:

> Edgar James Helms (1863–1942), a man admired for his uncommon character and entrepreneurial vision, is credited as the founder of the movement that would grow into Goodwill.
>
> Helms was born near Malone, New York, on January 19, 1863. As a young man, he had tried his hand at law and newspaper publishing, but felt called to the ministry. In 1889, he enrolled in Boston University Theological School.
>
> Helms and two fellow students requested that the City Missionary Society support them in opening a full-scale settlement house in the North End.
>
> Instead, Helms was offered a struggling inner city mission in Boston's South End, Morgan Chapel, established a generation earlier by Henry Morgan.
>
> The young minister was appalled at the conditions faced by immigrants who found themselves in a new country without jobs and sometimes desperate for food, clothing and shelter. Using burlap bags from Thomas Wood and Company, Helms went door-to-door in Boston's wealthiest districts asking for donations of clothing and household goods.

Helms' model differed from many charities of the day, emphasizing that donated goods could be sold for profit and that money would be used to pay workers who helped refurbish those goods. Helms hired people in need —many of whom were considered unemployable to do this repair work.

Employees were paid $4 a day. When money was scarce, workers were given $5 clothing vouchers.

Although it wasn't until 1915 that the term Goodwill Industries® was coined, 1902 became known as the year Goodwill was born. With the help of Methodist Church funding, Helms went on to help establish Goodwill organizations across the United States.

By 1920, there were 15 Goodwill organizations established, including Morgan Memorial Goodwill Industries in Boston.

Major economic and political crises like the financial crash of 1929, the Great Depression, and World War I solidified the need for an organization like Goodwill.

An estimated 1,500 people thronged Boston's Morgan Memorial Church of All Nations to pay final tribute at his funeral on December 27, 1942. Bishop G. Bromley Oxnam spoke these words in his eulogy:

"[Helms] was blessed with a fine mind, a great heart and a strong will. His unusual business ability, passionate devotion and physical strength enabled him to serve his fellow man, who were uninterested in charity, but yearned for a chance."

In 2002, during Goodwill's Centennial Celebration, a bronze medallion in Helms' honor was added to The Extra Mile — Points of Light Volunteer Pathway in Washington, D.C., the only national monument that honors individuals who selflessly championed causes to help others realize a better America.

Today, Goodwill sponsors two annual national awards that honor staff ... who exemplify Helms' values of unselfish service, self-reliance and a strong work ethic.

Reverend Edgar J. Helms gave an address at the Council of Cities, Baltimore, Maryland., April 26, 1918 (E.J. Helms, *Pioneering in Modern City Missions,* Boston, MA: Morgan Memorial Printing, 1927, chapter 3. "The Relation of the Church to Industrial Evangelism," p. 126–7).

> If the spirit of God is to dominate the whole social order, then must He be manifest as much in the family and industry and state as He is in the Church.
>
> The Church has a greater task of evangelism than to secure individuals who will lift their hands for prayer or sign a card or shake hands with an evangelist ...

Helms continued:

> Employer and employee must shake hands in mutual respect and cooperation. The era of exploitation and competition between nations and races must end in mutual helpfulness and goodwill. Jesus Christ and His Gospel must permeate industry and every human interest as well as preaching and education. The Church is His divinely appointed agency for this task.

In a 1935 training manual, Rev. R.E. Scully, head of Goodwill's Department of Religious and Cultural Work, wrote:

> The ideals of the Goodwill Industries are distinctly religious ... We seek to save the man, his self-respect, his morale, and his soul ... (with) spiritual encouragement, moral uplift, and Christian fellowship.

A.T. PIERSON: EVANGELIZE THE WORLD IN THIS GENERATION

Arthur Tappan Pierson was born in New York, March 6, 1837, in an apartment across from Charles Finney's Broadway Tabernacle. He corresponded with Finney, and stated at Finney's Memorial Service at Oberlin, July 28, 1876:

> Before my birth, for months my father and mother were in constant attendance on the services of Mr. Finney in the Chatham Street chapel, New York. They occupied the very house beneath which, by an archway, the throngs poured into the chapel.
>
> The impression then made upon my mother's mind, determined her to consecrate me to the work of the ministry; and from my birth I never knew any hour when I was converted, and when I did not expect to be a minister. (*Reminiscences of Charles G. Finney,* pp. 28-29.)

Arthur Tappan Pierson was named after the fiery New York anti-slavery abolitionist Arthur Tappan. His entire life, A.T. Pierson abhorred slavery, opposed southern convict-leasing and the colonial exploitation of native populations.

In 1850, at age 13, Pierson publicly professed faith in Jesus Christ at a Methodist revival.

At Hamilton College, Clinton, New York, he was an award winning orator, a Phi Beta Kappa student, and excelled in language, daily using Hebrew and Greek in his Scripture studies.

Graduating in 1857, A.T. Pierson was accepted into Union Theological Seminary, founded by nine Presbyterian ministers in 1836, being the oldest independent seminary in the U.S. He was one of the first one hundred members of the New York City Y.M.C.A. and had a passion for that organization his whole life.

During the 1857 Layman's Prayer Revival, he described experiences of the Holy Spirit. The impact on him was so profound that it swayed his classmate, George Edward Post, into becoming a medical missionary to Lebanon and Syria.

After graduation in 1860, A.T. Pierson married Sarah Frances Benedict, and together they had seven children, many of whom served as pastors, missionaries, or lay leaders.

He was ordained a Presbyterian minister and served at the First Congregational Church of Binghamton, New York, then the Presbyterian church in Waterford, New York.

In 1869, he became pastor of Fort Street Presbyterian Church of Detroit, Michigan. In

14 years, as he taught a weekly Bible Class and Teachers' Institute, it grew into one of the largest and wealthiest churches in the city.

Pierson helped found the Presbyterian Alliance to help needy churches, and the Tappan Presbyterian Association at the University of Michigan in Ann Arbor to reach students.

Then, at 40-years-old, being pastor of one of Detroit's most prominent churches, he had a self-reflective experience. During a six week revival in 1874, preached by evangelists Major D.W. Whittle and P.P. Bliss, he realized the pressing needs of church building inadvertently directed his attention into seeking approval of the affluent.

He repented and began to lead his congregation in reaching out to Detroit's poor. He ended the tradition of his church having a reliable income from pew rents and pioneered faith missions. Considering Matthew 28:19, "Go therefore and make disciples of all nations," he made it his goal to see the world evangelized in his generation.

In 1886, he wrote *The Crisis of Missions*,1886; *Evangelistic Work in Principle and Practice*, 1887; *The Divine Enterprise of Missions,* 1891; *Miracles of Missions – 4 vols.*, 1891–1901; and *The Modern Mission Century viewed as a Cycle of Divine Working*, 1901.

Beginning in 1888, he edited for the next 24 years the inter-denominational *Missionary Review of the World* and lectured on missions at Rutgers College, and was a delegate to the 1888 World Conference on Missions in London.

He made a missionary trip to the United Kingdom, 1889–1890, and in 1892, was a Duff lecturer in Scotland.

Pierson addressed the pivotal Ecumenical Conference on Foreign Missions in New York City, 1900. He was friends with Adoniram Judson Gordon, who spoke at D.L. Moody's revival meetings and founded Gordon–Conwell Theological Seminary to train missionaries.

He became friends with C.I. Scofield, and helped edit the *Scofield Reference Bible*, 1909.

Pierson met Pastor Charles Spurgeon, whose 6,000 seat Metropolitan Tabernacle in London was the largest non-conformist church of its day.

When Spurgeon, a Baptist, began to suffer from Bright's disease, he asked Pierson, a Presbyterian, to fill the pulpit. When Spurgeon, died on January 31, 1892, the church asked Pierson to stay.

Pierson wrote *From the Pulpit to the Palm–Branch: Memorial of Charles H. Spurgeon, 1892.*

Initially, his views on the mode of baptism were different, but on February 1, 1896, at the age of 58, he decided to be baptized by Spurgeon's brother, James A. Spurgeon.

Pierson befriended George Mueller, the director of the Ashley Down orphanage in Bristol, England, and wrote his biography, *George Muller of Bristol and his Witness to a Prayer–Hearing God* (1899).

Muller was a founder of the Plymouth Brethren, or Open Brethren, and spread the idea that Jews should begin a movement to reclaim their homeland. He influenced Pierson's eschatology to believe in the premillennial return of Jesus Christ. In 1896, Pierson wrote *The Coming of the Lord.*

Pierson was friends with D.L. Moody, and preached at his historic International Y.M.C.A. conference held at Moody's Northfield Mount Hermon School for Boys in 1881.

It was there that the young Y.M.C.A. leader from Cornell University, John R. Mott, heard Pierson's challenge and decided to dedicate his life to evangelizing the world in this generation. Mott made such a global impact that he was awarded the Nobel Peace Prize in 1946.

Dana L. Robert, Assistant Professor of Missions at Boston University School of Theology, wrote her Yale University Ph.D. dissertation *The Legacy of Arthur Tappan Pierson*, 1984, providing insights into A.T. Pierson.

In the 1880s, he ignited a great missionary movement among young people, the Student Volunteer Movement, "bringing the Gospel into contact with unsaved souls."

Acting as the movement's elder statesman, he put forth that missions should be the work of every single church, with the goal being "the evangelization of the world in this generation."

When Pierson was preaching a revival at Princeton University in 1886, a student, Robert E. Speer, heard his message and came to faith in Christ. Speer became secretary of the Presbyterian Board of Foreign Missions in 1891, then served as a missionary in Persia, India, China, Korea, Japan, and South America.

Speer credited Pierson with being the greatest popularizer of missions of the age.

Pierson was friends with J. Hudson Taylor, founder of the China Inland Mission. He helped establish the Africa Inland Mission and advocated for "faith missions" to build indigenous churches.

He influenced Samuel Zwemer to be a missionary to the Islamic world, including Busrah, Iraq, Arabia, and to found the American Mission Hospital in Bahrain. He motivated Horace Grant Underwood to spread Christianity in Korea.

Then a liberal movement called "Modernism" began to sweep through mainline seminaries throwing cold water on sending missionaries, suggesting instead that Bible beliefs were not fixed but should be adjusted every time a new scientific theory became popular.

Pierson led the opposition to this, publishing a series of apologetic booklets called *The Fundamentals*, defending Biblical orthodoxy against critics. For this, Pierson was labeled the "Father of Fundamentalism" and those siding with him "Fundamentalists."

The Fundamentalist–Modernist Controversy forced churches to choose sides between a "woke" watered down understanding of the Bible or committing to inerrant Bible orthodoxy. Liberals accommodated evolution while Pierson advocated day-age creationism.

A.T. Pierson wrote *Many Infallible Proofs: Chapters on the Evidences of Christianity,* 1886; and *The Bible and Spiritual Criticism,* 1906.

In one of his best-selling books, *In Christ Jesus: or, The Sphere of the Believer's Life,* 1898, he explained the phrase "in Christ Jesus," a preposition followed by a proper name, was key to understanding the New Testament.

Pierson spoke at the Keswick Convention,

highlighting the vital importance of work of the Holy Spirit in a believer's life. He wrote; *The Keswick Movement in Precept and Practice,* (1903); *Acts of the Holy Spirit,* (1895); *New Acts of the Apostles,* (1894); *LifePower: or, Character Culture, and Conduct,* (1895); and *Catharine of Siena, an ancient Lay Preacher,* (1898).

In 1910, Pierson traveled to Korea where he spoke at Namdaemoon Church. His visit established the Pierson Memorial Union Bible Institute, today Pyeongtaek University, in 1912. Many renowned pastors and scholars attended there.

A.T. Pierson died in 1911. During his lifetime, he wrote over 50 books, preached over 13,000 sermons, and gave lectures around the world at missions and Bible conferences. On his gravestone is an open Bible engraved with two verses.

I John 5:11 "God hath given to us eternal life, and this life is in His Son."

Matthew 28:19 "Go ye therefore, and teach all nations, baptizing them in the name of the Father, and of the Son, and of the Holy Ghost."

JOHN R. MOTT, Y.M.C.A. WORLD COMMITTEE

John Raleigh Mott was born in Livingston Manor, New York, on May 25, 1865, the only son of four children.

That same year, his pioneer parents, John and

Elmira Mott, moved their family to Postville, Iowa, where his father worked as a lumber merchant and the town's first mayor.

At age 16, John Mott enrolled in Upper Iowa University, a small Methodist preparatory school in Fayette, Iowa. He excelled in history and literature, and became an award-winning orator and debater.

In 1885, he transferred to Cornell University to pursue his life's goal of either working in his father's lumber business or practicing law.

This all changed in one day, January 14, 1886, when one of his professors, J. Kynaston Studd, concluded his lecture, saying:

> Young man, seekest thou great things for thyself? Seek them not. "Seek ye first the Kingdom of God."

In a moment, Mott life's goal shifted. He decided his purpose was to present Christ to as many students as possible. He became president of Cornell University's Y.M.C.A. chapter, tripling its membership, and raised funds for a Y.M.C.A. campus building.

In the summer of 1886, Mott went as a Y.M.C.A. representative to the first-ever international Christian student conference, held at evangelist Dwight L. Moody's Mount Hermon School for Boys in Massachusetts.

In attendance were 251 college-age men from 89 colleges and universities, belonging to different denominations. On the final day of the conference, a Princeton graduate, Robert Parmelee Wilder, who had been raised by his missionary parents in India, gave an appeal for students to make a personal commitment to let the Lord use them in world missions.

One hundred, including John Mott, signed the Princeton Pledge, which declared;

> We hold ourselves willing and desirous to do the Lord's work wherever He may call us, even if it be in the foreign lands.

These young men became known as the "Mount Hermon Hundred." With the help of Arthur Tappan Pierson, they organized themselves into the Student Volunteer Movement for Foreign Missions in 1886.

Mott served as the chairman of its executive committee, and in the following two decades, over 20,000 young people were sent as missionaries around the world, considered one of the most significant events in mission history.

In 1888, Mott graduated from Cornell with a degree in history and philosophy, being a member of the prestigious Phi Beta Kappa, the oldest honor society in America.

In September of that year, he became national secretary of the Intercollegiate Y.M.C.A. of the U.S.A. and Canada, a position he held for the next 27 years, visiting colleges and challenging students to Christian service.

During this time he met Swedish Y.M.C.A. leader Karl Fries, who had organized the 1888 Y.M.C.A. World Conference in Stockholm.

Fries later became the general secretary of the Y.M.C.A. at its international headquarters in Geneva, Switzerland.

In 1891, Mott married teacher Leila Ada White of Wooster, Ohio. They had two sons and two daughters.

In 1895, Mott and Karl Fries of Sweden, organized the World's Student Christian Federation, with Mott serving as general secretary.

For the next two years, they traveled and organized Christian student movements in India, China, Japan, Australia, New Zealand, parts of Europe and the North East.

In 1900, Mott published his best-selling book, *The Evangelization of the World in this Generation*. This title was inspired by Arthur Tappan Pierson, and was the motto of the Student Volunteer movement in the early 20th century.

In April 1901, Mott spoke to students about their responsibility for evangelizing:

> The last command of Christ is operative until it is repealed. It is not optional, as some would assume, but obligatory. It awaits its fulfillment by a generation which shall have the requisite faith and courage, and audacity and the purpose of heart to do their duty to the whole world.

In 1910, Mott, as an American Methodist layperson, presided over the World Missionary Conference in Edinburgh, considered a milestone event in modern Protestant missions. He also was chairman of the International Missionary Council.

In 1912, Mott and a colleague were offered free passage from England to New York on the plush *Titanic* by a White Star Line official supporting their work. They declined, choosing to travel instead on the lower-class the *SS Lapland*.

C. Howard Hopkins, who wrote the biography, *John R. Mott, 1865–1955* (Eerdmans, 1980), that when the two men arrived in New York City and heard about the fate of the *Titanic*, they looked at each other and exclaimed, "The Good Lord must have more work for us to do."

Mott encouraged churches of all denominations to work together to reach the world for Christ.

After Europe, Mott traveled to Asia from October 1912 to May 1913. He held dozens of missionary conferences in Ceylon, India, Burma, Malaya, China, Korea and Japan.

After the Russian Revolution, with the help of Episcopal layman Robert Hallowell Gardiner III, Mott maintained relations with the Russian Orthodox Church.

In 1915, Mott became General Secretary of the International Y.M.C.A. Committee.

During World War I, he arranged for the Y.M.C.A. to assist President Woodrow Wilson in organizing Christian aid and relief work with prisoners of war. He was awarded the Distinguished Service Medal for his efforts serving as general secretary of the National War Work Council.

Mott declined President Wilson's offer to be ambassador to China, though he agreed to be a member of the Mexican Commission in 1916, and a Special Diplomatic Mission to Russia in 1917.

In 1920, Mott organized the World Student Christian Federation with societies involving over

3,000 schools around the globe. Thousands of college students of different denominations were mobilized to take the Gospel to the world. He served as the organization's chairman until 1928.

From 1926 to 1937, he was president of the Y.M.C.A.'s World Committee. In the inter-war years, Mott criticized the oppression of colonized peoples and pioneered efforts in the struggle against racial discrimination.

> I have tried to help weave together all countries, all races of mankind and all the Christian communities.

During WWII, he spearheaded Y.M.C.A. Relief operations for prisoners of war.

For his work in evangelism and ecumenism, many considered him "the most widely traveled and universally trusted Christian leader of his time."

He was awarded the Nobel Peace Prize in 1946. In his Acceptance Speech in Oslo, December 10, 1946, he stated:

> My life has been a life of travel – for 60 years ... journeys which ... have taken me to 83 countries ... In this world-wide effort I have concentrated on successive generations of youth.
>
> If I were to add a word, it would be a word of abounding hope. The present new generation ... (is) planning, as no previous generation, for a great united advance in the furtherance of peace and good-will throughout the world.

The New York Times published "WORLD'S LEADERS ACCLAIM DR. MOTT; Truman

Hails His Efforts to Spread Good-Will," December 20, 1946, in which Truman gave praise:

> Perhaps no man has labored more assiduously than you in the promotion of international good-will.

In 1948, Mott helped form the World Council of Churches, and was elected honorary President.

John and Leila Mott's son, John Livingstone Mott, worked with the Y.M.C.A. in India, being awarded by Britain's King George V with the Kaisar-i-Hind Medal for Public Service in India, 1931.

Their daughter, Irene Mott Bose served as a social worker in India, and married Indian Supreme Court justice Vivian Bose.

Leila Mott died in 1952. The following year, John Mott married Agnes Peter. She had worked with the Y.M.C.A. in France during World War I, caring for refugees and soldiers, and did this again during World War II.

Agnes was the first woman in France to be awarded the silver Medal of Honor. Agnes Peter was also a great-great-great granddaughter of Martha Washington.

John Mott died in 1955 at his home in Orlando, Florida, at the age of 89. He had stated:

> I have a hard fight before me in crushing self but it must and will be done. I shall be wholly consecrated and strive to be like Christ.

During his lifetime, Mott gave thousands of speeches and chaired hundreds of conferences and committees. He crisscrossed the Pacific Ocean 14 times and the Atlantic over 100 times. For nearly

50 years, he averaged 34 days a year at sea.

He received honorary University degrees from Yale, Princeton, Brown, Edinburgh, Toronto, and Upper Iowa; and the Russian Orthodox Church of Paris. He was awarded honors from: China, Czechoslovakia, Finland, France, Greece, Hungary, Italy, Japan, Jerusalem, Poland, Portugal, Siam, Sweden, and the United States.

His papers are held at the Yale Divinity School Library. His books include:

The Decisive Hour of Christian Missions (1910)

World Student Christian Federation (1920)

Cooperation and the World Mission (1935)

Methodists United for Action (1939)

The Larger Evangelism (1945)

John R. Mott stated in his Nobel Lecture "The Leadership Demanded in This Momentous Time," December 13, 1946:

> There is an irresistible demand to strengthen the leadership of the constructive forces of the world at the present momentous time ...
>
> The summons has come to wage a better planned, more aggressive, and more triumphant warfare against the age-long enemies of mankind – ignorance, poverty, disease, strife, and sin ... of divisive influences on every hand ... Of these divisive manifestations has been ... race relations. In some respects this has become most serious because most neglected ...
>
> Bishop Gorel ... summed up our need ... "We do not think and we do not pray"; that

is, we do not use the principal power at our disposal – the power of thought – and we do not avail ourselves of incomparably our greatest power – the superhuman power of prayer. Well may we heed the injunction of St. Peter to "gird up the loins of your mind."

How essential it is that those who tomorrow are to lead ... that the discipline of their lives, the culture of their souls, and the thoroughness of their processes of spiritual discovery and appropriations be such as will enable them to meet the demands of a most exacting age.

The leadership must be statesmanlike. And here let us remind ourselves of the traits of the true statesman – the genuinely Christian statesman. He simply must be a man of vision ... How true it is that where there is no vision the people perish.

The most trustworthy leader is one who adopts and applies guiding principles. He trusts them like the North Star. He follows his principles no matter how many oppose him and no matter how few go with him ...

A most highly multiplying trait in point of far-reaching influences is that of ability to discover and use strong men ...

Mott continued:

Of front line importance among the most contagious and enduring traits of the leaders of nations and of all callings is that of spotless character.

How this stands out in the chapter on "Aristides the Just" in Plutarch. And how the opposite stands out in Lorenzo de' Medici of whom it was said that "he was cultured yet corrupt, wise yet cruel, spending the morning writing a verse in praise of virtue and spending the night in vice."

Among the qualities most needed among those who aspire to true leadership in the fostering of peace and goodwill among the nations and in overcoming racial and religious antagonism is the cooperative spirit and objective ...

In common with Christians the world over, I would gratefully acknowledge the heroic and truly Christian guidance and backing afforded by Lutheran Bishop Elvin Berggrav of Oslo and other leaders of the church. [who resisted Nazi invasion and defended rights of Jews] ...

In closing, let me emphasize the all-important point that Jesus Christ summed up the outstanding, unfailing, and abiding secret of all truly great and enduring leadership in the Word: "He who would be greatest among you shall be the servant of all."

He Himself embodied this truth and became "the Prince Leader of the Faith", that is, the leader of the leaders.

LORD BADEN POWELL FOUNDED THE BOY SCOUTS

The self-reliance of muscular Christianity was embodied in the Y.M.C.A.'s Boys Work Department, organized in 1869 by William H. Whipple in Salem, Massachusetts, with "regular and successful religious meetings for boys."

The earliest record of Boys Work camping is in the 1860s. The Vermont Y.M.C.A. boys missionary, later called "secretary," took boys on summer camping trips to Lake Champlain. Other chapters followed the example.

In 1885, Y.M.C.A. volunteer Sumner F. Dudley began a summer camp for boys 12 to 18 years old. It was so successful, he expanded it, resulting in him being called "father of organized camping." The Y.M.C.A. named its first permanent summer camp after him, Camp Dudley, 625 acres located near Westport, New York. It is the oldest continuously running camp in America.

In 1892, Dudley was hired as part-time Y.M.C.A. Boys Work secretary to organize some 30,000 boys. In 1900, Edgar M. Robinson was hired as full-time secretary of the Y.M.C.A. Boys Work Department, which was described as "a definite Christian program of character discussions, hikes, debating, clean living campaigns, and leadership and service tasks."

In the next decade Y.M.C.A. Boys Work grew to 120,000 boys with 187 camps, later called "Hi-Y." B.M. Russell, the Y.M.C.A. Boys Work secretary in Providence, Rhode Island, organized a father-son banquet with 300 participants in 1909. It was the first of its kind, and within a few decades, over 3 million were participating.

In England, a person supportive of the Y.M.C.A. Boys Work camps was Lord Baden Powell, a war hero recently returned from the South African Boer War. Educated at Charterhouse, London, he joined the English hussars in 1876, and served throughout the British Empire – the largest empire in world history. He was stationed in India, Afghanistan and South Africa.

In 1895, he commanded native troops in Ashanti–Ghana, where he opposed the slave trade. He served in the Matabele–Zimbabwe campaign.

Dr. David Livingstone, Scottish missionary to the Congo, 1841–1873, also condemned the slave trade, giving a shocking, an eye-witness account of a Muslim-led caravan of 1,000 black slaves shackled together with neck yokes and leg irons, forced to march single file 500 miles to the sea, carrying heavy loads of ivory.

Livingstone wrote to the *New York Herald*:

> If my disclosures regarding the terrible Ujijian slavery should lead to the suppression of the East Coast slave trade, I shall regard that as a greater matter by far than the discovery of all the Nile sources together.

Another notable young British soldier at this time was Winston Churchill. He was stationed in Cuba, India, Egypt, Sudan, then went as a correspondent to South Africa during the Second Boer War. He was captured, escaped, made a cavalry lieutenant, and helped capture Pretoria.

Churchill described Pakistan and Afghanistan in *The Story of the Malakand Field Force* (1898):

> The Mad Mullah was ... a wild enthusiast ... preached a crusade, or Jehad, against the infidel ... It is ... impossible for the modern European to fully appreciate the force

which fanaticism exercises ... Tribesmen become convulsed in an ecstasy of religious bloodthirstiness ... Only those who had doubted had perished, said the Mullah.

In the Second South African Boer War, Baden-Powell's 1,200 men were besieged for 217 days by an overwhelming Boer army of 8,000 at Mafeking. In the face of famine and sickness, his resourcefulness successfully defended their position, saving his men until help arrived, May 12, 1900. The British won the Boer Wars, but it signaled the start of the decline of their Empire.

Baden-Powell was promoted to Major General and returned to England in 1903 as a war hero. He was pleasantly surprised to find the Y.M.C.A. Boys Work had been using his soldiers survival aid manual. The Y.M.C.A. sponsored Baden-Powell on a promotional lecture tour.

The Y.M.C.A. supported Baden-Powell's first trial boys camp on Brownsea Island, and formed joint scout troops with him.

In 1908, Baden-Powell published *Scouting for Boys,* which sold 150 million copies, becoming the 4th best-selling book of the 20th century.

In it, he wrote:

> No man is much good unless he believes in God and obeys His laws ... First: Love and serve God. Second: Love and serve your neighbor.

Baden-Powell officially founded the Boy Scouts in 1908, with the purpose being to instill in young men the qualities of morality, self-reliance, resourcefulness, outdoorsmanship, and good citizenship He wrote in *Scouting for Boys:*

> We aim for the practice of Christianity in their everyday life and dealings, and not merely the profession of its theology on Sundays ...
>
> There is a vast reserve of loyal patriotism and Christian spirit lying dormant in our nation today, mainly because it sees no direct opportunity for expressing itself ...
>
> In this joyous brotherhood there is vast opportunity open to all ... It gives every man his chance of service for his fellow-men and for God.

On February 8, 1910, newspaper publisher William D. Boyce incorporated the Boy Scouts of America, with its first headquarters being in the Y.M.C.A. office in New York. The Boy Scouts of America grew significantly when merged with Ernest Thompson Seton's Woodcraft Indians, and Dan Beard's Society of the Sons of Daniel Boone.

It grew even more when the Y.M.C.A. Boys Work secretary in Chicago, Edgar Robinson, who was overseeing a national membership of some 120,000 boys, agreed to be the first national director of the Boy Scouts of America. Y.M.C.A. leaders joined in organizing Boy Scout troops.

Since its founding in 1910, the Boy Scouts of America has had an estimate 130 million boys participate, along with 465,000 adult volunteers.

In 1914, Britain entered World War I. Baden-Powell visited Y.M.C.A. huts on the Western Front. He raised support for them by writing an article in *The YM British Empire Weekly.*

He appealed to Lord Edmund Allenby for help funding the Y.M.C.A.'s work with soldiers.

On October 7, 1915, Baden-Powell funded a Y.M.C.A. hut at Val-de-Lievre, near Calais, and his wife Olave helped staff it. On January 1, 1916, the Baden-Powells opened another Y.M.C.A. hut at Etaples, with money raised by the Boy Scouts

Baden-Powell toured England with Y.M.C.A.'s General Secretary Sir Arthur Keysall Yapp to appeal for funds. He wrote a chapter of the Y.M.C.A. book, *Told in the Huts*, 1916.

In his 1917 pamphlet *Scouting & Christianity*, Baden-Powell wrote in the introduction:

> Scouting is nothing less than applied Christianity.

He wrote in *Aids to Scoutmastership*, 1919:

> Development of outlook naturally begins with a respect for God ... Reverence to God and reverence for one's neighbor and reverence for oneself as a servant of God.

In 1910, Baden-Powell helped his sister, Agnes Baden-Powell found Girl Guides. In 1912, he married Olave St. Clair Soames, and in 1939 they moved to a cottage in Kenya.

During this time, other boys organization were formed in England, such as: Boy's Life Brigade in 1890, with a naval sea branch called Life Boys; British Boy Scouts in 1909; National Peace Scouts in 1910; Order of World Scouts in 1911, and Boys Brigade founded 1926.

The Boy Scouts went on to be the world's largest voluntary youth movement, with an estimated 500 million boys and adults participating since its founding in 1908.

Sir Robert Baden-Powell's works include:
Cavalry Instruction, 1885;
The Matabele Campaign, 1896;
Scouting for Boys, 1908;
The Handbook for the Girl Guides, co-authored with Agnes Baden-Powell, 1912;
Boy Scouts Beyond The Sea: My World Tour, 1913;
My Adventures as a Spy, 1915;
Memories of India, 1915;
Young Knights of the Empire, 1916;
The Wolf Cub's Handbook, 1916;
Girl Guiding, 1918;
Aids To Scoutmastership, 1919:
What Scouts Can Do: More Yarns, 1921:
An Old Wolf's Favourites, 1921;
Rovering to Success, 1922;
Life's Snags and How to Meet Them, 1927;
Scouting and Youth Movements, 1929;
Last Message to Scouts, 1929;
He-who-sees-in-the-dark; The Boys' Story of Frederick Burnham, the American Scout, 1932;
Lessons From the Varsity of Life, 1933;
Adventures and Accidents, 1934;
Scouting Round the World, 1935;
Adventuring to Manhood, 1936;
African Adventures, 1937;
Birds and Beasts of Africa, 1938
Paddle Your Own Canoe, 1939;
More Sketches Of Kenya, 1940.

Sir Robert Baden-Powell died January 8, 1941. Among his papers was found an envelope marked "in the event of my death" with the message:

> To my Brother Scouters and Guides: I have had an extraordinary experience in seeing the development of Scouting from its beginning up to its present stage ...
>
> I have been lucky enough to find you men and women to form a group of the right stamp who can be relied upon to carry it on to its goal.
>
> You will do well to keep your eyes open, in your turn, for worthy successors to who you can, with confidence, hand on the torch.
>
> Don't let it become a salaried organization: keep it a voluntary movement of patriotic service ...
>
> Its aim is to produce healthy, happy, helpful citizens, of both sexes, to eradicate the prevailing narrow self-interest; personal, political, sectarian and national, and to substitute for it a broader spirit of self-sacrifice and service in the cause of humanity; and thus to develop mutual goodwill and cooperation not only within our own country but abroad, between all countries ... This consummation is no idle or fantastic dream, but is a practicable possibility – if we work for it ...
>
> Hundreds of thousands of boys and girls who are learning our ideals today will be the fathers and mothers of millions in the near future, in whom they will in turn inculcate the same ideals – provided that these are really and unmistakably impressed upon

them by the leaders of today ...

You, who are Scouters and Guiders, are not only doing a great work for your neighbor's children, but are also helping in practical fashion to bring to pass God's Kingdom of peace and goodwill upon earth. So, from my heart, I wish you Godspeed in your effort. — Baden-Powell

BOY SCOUTS OF AMERICA

In 1911, the Boy Scouts of America sought a permanent Chief Scout Executive. Y.M.C.A. director Dr. Luther Gulick suggested James E. West.

West had served as general secretary of the Y.M.C.A. during the Spanish–American War. He became a Washington, D.C. attorney and helped established the juvenile court system.

In 1902, President Theodore Roosevelt appointed him to the Department of the Interior Board of Pension Appeals. He served as secretary of the Playground Association of America.

West served as the BSA Chief Scout Executive for the next 32 years. He added the last three points to the Scout Law: "brave, clean, and reverent," and the line in the Scout Oath:

> To help other people at all times, to keep myself physically strong, mentally awake and morally straight.

He published the first edition of *The Official*

Handbook for Boys.

As the Boy Scouts of America was closely associated with the Y.M.C.A, which was known as a Protestant Christian organization, many Catholic churches discouraged boys from joining. Beginning in 1913, West promoted the Boy Scouts as non-sectarian, resulting in Catholics joining.

Prior to World War I, there was a pacifism versus patriotism conflict in America. Pacifists accused Boy Scouts of being semi-militaristic due to its uniforms and discipline. West caved to the pressure and deemphasized training youth with rifles and ended the Marksmanship Merit Badge.

When a pacifist article was published in the *Boy Life Magazine* in 1914, Major General Dr. Leonard Wood protested by resigning from the Boy Scout board. Wood was a Medal of Honor recipient, and personal physician to Presidents Cleveland and McKinley. He served in the U.S. Army during the Spanish–American War, commanding the Rough Riders with Theodore Roosevelt as his second-in-command.

Wood had been Chief of Staff of the U.S. Army, Military Governor of Cuba, and Governor-General of the Philippines.

When Theodore Roosevelt became aware of the situation, he contacted James West and persuaded him to move from pacifism to patriotism. West then reemphasized the Marksmanship merit badge.

This is the letter from Theodore Roosevelt, Honorary Vice-president, Boy Scouts of America to Mr. James E. West, Executive Secretary, Boy Scouts of America, New York City.

My Dear Sir ... the Boy Scout Movement is of peculiar importance to the whole country. It has already done much good, and it will do far more, for it is in its essence a practical scheme through which to impart a proper standard of ethical conduct, proper standards of fair play and consideration for others, and courage and decency, to boys who have never been reached and never will be reached by the ordinary type of preaching, lay or clerical.

I have been particularly interested in that extract of a letter from a scout master in the Philippines (Elwood Brown) which runs as follows:

"It might interest you to know that at a recent fire in Manila which devastated acres of ground and rendered 3,000 people homeless, that two patrols of the Manila scouts reached the fire almost with the fire companies, reported to the proper authorities and worked for hours under very trying conditions helping frightened natives into places of safety, removing valuables and other articles from houses that apparently were in the path of the flames, and performing cheerfully and efficiently all the tasks given to them by the firemen and scout master. They were complimented in the public press, and in a kind editorial about their work." ...

What these Boy Scouts of the Philippines have just done, I think our Boy Scouts in every town and country district should train themselves to be able to do.

The movement is one for efficiency

and patriotism. It does not try to make soldiers of Boy Scouts, but to make boys who will turn out as men to be fine citizens, and who will, if their country needs them, make better soldiers for having been scouts.

Theodore Roosevelt continued:

> No one can be a good American unless he is a good citizen, and every boy ought to train himself so that as a man he will be able to do his full duty to the community.
>
> I want to see the Boy Scouts not merely utter fine sentiments, but act on them; not merely sing, "My Country 'Tis of Thee," but act in a way that will give them a country to be proud of.
>
> No man is a good citizen unless he so acts as to show that he actually uses the Ten Commandments, and translates the Golden Rule into his life conduct – and I don't mean by this in exceptional cases under spectacular circumstances, but I mean applying the Ten Commandments and the Golden Rule in the ordinary affairs of every-day life.
>
> I hope the Boy Scouts will practice truth and square dealing, and courage and honesty, so that when as young men they begin to take a part not only in earning their own livelihood, but in governing the community, they may be able to show in practical fashion their insistence upon the great truth that the eighth and ninth commandments are directly related to every-day life, not only between men as such in their private relations, but between men

and the government of which they are part.

Indeed the boys, even while only boys, can have a very real effect upon the conduct of the grown up members of the community. For decency and square dealing are just as contagious as vice and corruption.

Every healthy boy ought to feel and will feel that in order to amount to anything, it is necessary to have a constructive, and not merely a destructive nature; and if he can keep this feeling as he grows up, he has taken his first step toward good citizenship.

The man who tears down and criticizes and scolds may be a good citizen, but only in a negative sense; and if he never does anything else, he is apt not to be a good citizen at all.

The man who counts, and the boy who counts, are the man and boy who steadily endeavor to build up, to improve, to better living conditions everywhere and all about them.

But the boy can do an immense amount right in the present, entirely aside from training himself to be a good citizen in the future; and he can only do this if he associates himself with other boys. Let the Boy Scouts see to it that the best use is made of the parks and playgrounds in their villages and home towns.

A gang of toughs may make a playground impossible; and if the boy scouts in the neighborhood of that particular playground are fit for their work, they will show that they won't permit any such gang of toughs to have its way ...

I hope, by the way, that one of the

prime teachings among the Boy Scouts will be the teaching against vandalism.

Let it be a point of honor to protect birds, trees and flowers, and so to make our country more beautiful and not more ugly, because we have lived in it. The same qualities that mean success or failure to the nation as a whole, mean success or failure in men and boys individually.

The Boy Scouts must war against the same foes and vices that most hurt the nation; and they must try to develop the same virtues that the nation most needs.

To be helpless, self-indulgent, or wasteful, will turn the boy into a mighty poor kind of a man, just as the indulgence in such vices by the men of a nation means the ruin of the nation.

Let the boy stand stoutly against his enemies both from without and from within, let him show courage in confronting fearlessly one set of enemies, and in controlling and mastering the others.

Any boy is worth nothing if he has not got courage, courage to stand up against the forces of evil, and courage to stand up in the right path. Let him be unselfish and gentle, as well as strong and brave.

It should be a matter of pride to him that he is not afraid of anyone, and that he scorns not to be gentle and considerate to everyone, and especially to those who are weaker than he is.

If he doesn't treat his mother and sisters well, then he is a poor creature no matter what else he does; just as a man who doesn't treat his wife well is a poor kind of citizen no matter what his other qualities may be.

And, by the way, don't ever forget to let the boy know that courtesy, politeness, and good manners must not be neglected. They are not little things, because they are used at every turn in daily life.

Let the boy remember also that in addition to courage, unselfishness, and fair dealing, he must have efficiency, he must have knowledge, he must cultivate a sound body and a good mind, and train himself so that he can act with quick decision in any crisis that may arise.

Mind, eye, muscle, all must be trained so that the boy can master himself, and thereby learn to master his fate. I heartily wish all good luck to the movement.

Very sincerely yours,
Theodore Roosevelt, The Outlook, 287 Fourth Avenue, New York, Office of Theodore Roosevelt, July 20th, 1911.

West did not favor the Girl Scouts, but rather supported the Camp Fire Girls, founded by his friends, Dr. Luther and Lottie Gulick.

West changed his views when President Herbert Hoover's wife, First Lady Louise Hoover, became the leader of the Girl Scouts.

Regarding faith, the *Scout Handbook, 5th edition*, 1948, explained "A Scout is Reverent":

The Scout shows true reverence in two principal ways.

First, you pray to God, you love God and you serve Him. Secondly, in your everyday actions you help other people, because they are made by God to God's own likeness.

You and all men are made by God to God's own likeness. You and all men are important in the sight of God because God made you.

The "unalienable rights" in our historic Declaration of Independence, come from God. That is why you respect others whose religion and customs may differ from yours.

The Scout Handbook, 5th edition, 1948, in the section "Duty to God," a scout was admonished to be "faithful to God's Commandments":

You worship God regularly with your family in your church or synagogue. You try to follow the religious teachings that you have been taught, and you are faithful in your church school duties, and help in church activities.

Above all you are faithful to Almighty God's Commandments.

Most great men in history have been men of deep religious faith. Washington knelt in the snow to pray at Valley Forge. Lincoln always sought Divine guidance before each important decision.

Be proud of your religious faith. Remember in doing your duty to God, to be grateful to Him. Whenever you succeed in doing something well, thank Him for it.

Sometimes when you look up into the starlit sky on a quiet night, and feel close to Him—thank Him as the Giver of all good things.

One way to express your duty and your thankfulness to God is to help others, and this too, is a part of your Scout Promise.

Many Presidents addressed the Boy Scouts.

On May 1, 1919, President Woodrow Wilson proclaimed a National Boy Scout Week:

> The Boy Scout movement should not only be preserved, but strengthened. It deserves the support of all public-spirited citizens ...
>
> Every nation depends for its future upon the proper training and development of its youth.

On July 25, 1924, President Calvin Coolidge addressed a gathering of Boy Scouts in New York headed to Copenhagen:

> The three fundamentals of scouthood are reverence for nature... reverence for law ... reverence for God. It is hard to see how a great man can be an atheist.
>
> Without the sustaining influence of faith in a divine power we could have little faith in ourselves ...
>
> Doubters do not achieve; skeptics do not contribute; cynics do not create.
>
> Faith is the great motive power, and no man realizes his full possibilities unless he has the deep conviction that life is eternally important, and that his work, well done, is part of an unending plan.

Coolidge addressed the National Council of Boy Scouts of America, May 1, 1926:

> We are delighted to honor this evening, Sir Robert Baden-Powell. This distinguished British general is now known all over the world ...

> It has been dignified by a Federal charter granted by the Congress to the Boy Scouts of America in 1916, and thereby ranks in the popular mind with the only two other organizations which have been similarly honored, the Red Cross and the American Legion ...
>
> The boy on becoming a scout binds himself on his honor to do his best ...
>
> 1. To do my duty to God and my country, and to obey the Scout Law.
> 2. To help other people at all times.
> 3. To keep myself physically strong, mentally awake, and morally straight.

He continued:

> The 12 articles in these Scout Laws are ... affirmative rules of conduct.
>
> Members must promise to be trustworthy, loyal, helpful, friendly, courteous, kind, obedient, cheerful, thrifty, brave, clean, and reverent. How comprehensive this list! What a formula for developing moral and spiritual character! ...
>
> It would be a perfect world if everyone exemplified these virtues ...
>
> Boys are taught to practice the basic virtues and principles of right living and to act for themselves in according such virtues and principles. They learn ... self-control ...
>
> We hear much talk of the decline in the influence of religion, of the loosening of the home ties, of the lack of discipline — all tending to break down reverence and respect for the laws of

God and man ...

There is no substitute for the influences of the home and of religion. These take hold of the innermost nature of the individual and play a very dominant part in the formation of personality and character ... Nothing else can ever take its place ...

Coolidge added:

The Boy Scout movement can never be ... a substitute but ... an ally of strict parental control and family life under religious influences ... The last item in the Scout "duodecalogue" is impressive. It declares that a scout shall be reverent. "He is reverent toward God," the paragraph reads. "He is faithful in his religious duties, and respects the convictions of others in matters of custom and religion."

In the past I have declared my conviction that our Government rests upon religion; that religion is the source from which we derive our reverence for truth and justice, for equality and liberty, and for the rights of mankind ...

The Boy Scout movement designed that the various religious denominations have found it a most helpful agency ...

We know too well what fortune overtakes those who attempt to live in opposition to these standards. They become ... outlaws.

However much they may boast of their freedom from all restraints ... they are immediately the recognized foes

... Their short existence is lived under greater and greater restrictions, in terror of the law, in flight from arrest, or in imprisonment.

Instead of gaining freedom, they become slaves of their own evil doing, realizing the scriptural assertion that they who sin are the servants of sin and that the wages of sin is death.

The Boy Scout movement has been instituted in order that the youth, instead of falling under the domination of habits and actions that lead only to destruction, may come under the discipline of a training that leads to eternal life.

President Franklin D. Roosevelt emphasized "moral responsibility," February 8, 1939:

These boys, so full of promise for the future ... should be regarded as a national trust.

Ours is the duty to inculcate in the Scout mind those simple but fundamental principles which embrace strength of body, alertness of mind and, above these and growing out of them, that sense of moral responsibility upon which all sound character rests.

President Roosevelt greeted the Boy Scouts, February 8, 1940:

Boy Scouts ... is ... truly American. God grant that it may ever remain so ...

Our 12th Scout Law effectively expresses the spiritual ideals of scouting ... It affirms the importance of religion in the life of the individual and the life of the nation and emphasizes the necessity of respect for the convictions of other people. Religious freedom is basic in Americanism. It is a tradition upon which our country is founded.

Roosevelt told the Scouts, February 7, 1943:

> Certainly those who help to make boys physically strong, mentally awake, and morally straight in these times deserve the appreciation of all who are leaders in America.

Franklin Roosevelt broadcast over radio, February 10, 1934:

> I am happy to participate in the 24th Anniversary Celebration of ... the Boy Scouts of America ...
>
> I ask you to join with me ... All stand! Give the Scout sign! Repeat with me the Scout Oath!
>
> "On my honor I will do my best: To do my duty to God and my country and to obey the Scout Law; To help other people at all times; To keep myself physically strong, mentally awake, and morally straight."

President Eisenhower said on the 50th Anniversary of the Boy Scouts of America, June 1, 1960:

> That is the great thing about Scouting ... We read in our Bibles the Parable of the Good Samaritan ... They individually and collectively begin to think of their nation in part as a "good Samaritan," doing the decent thing in this world ..
>
> Scouting is indeed doing something

... vital to our vigor as a nation based upon a religious concept.

Eisenhower told the 44th National Council of the Boy Scouts of America, May 29, 1954:

> It would be difficult for any political party or any government to state its purposes ... in better terms than ... the Scout Oath — "To do my duty by my God and country."
>
> One of my great heroes of American history is Robert E. Lee, and he said ...
>
> "We cannot do more than our duty. We would not wish to do less" ...
>
> Was there ever a time ... when we needed to be more ... morally straight?
>
> This Government, represented in its Legislature and its Executive departments and its Judiciary, has but one great purpose in its relationships with all other nations: to be morally straight.

President Gerald Ford stated at a Question-and-Answer Session at the Annual Convention of the Society of Professional Journalists, Sigma Delta Chi, Phoenix, Arizona, November 14, 1974:

> Q. Mr. President ... Senator Dole suggested that you shed your Boy Scout image and get tough with Congress and, if necessary, go over their heads ... What will be your tactics?
>
> THE PRESIDENT. Well, let me preface the answer ... I was a Boy Scout. I am proud of that experience. I have no apologies for it. I think they have done a great deal of good for lots of young people, and I am not going to back off from the 5

or 6 years that I enjoyed being a Boy Scout and doing the things that I think are good for America.

Now, to answer your other question. I wish there would be a lot more Boy Scouts.

President Ford remarked at the Boy Scouts Annual Awards Dinner, December 2, 1974:

It has recently been said that I am too much of a Boy Scout in the way I have conducted myself as President, and so I reviewed the Boy Scout Laws and Boy Scout Oath.

They say that a Scout is "trustworthy, loyal, helpful, friendly, courteous, kind, obedient, cheerful, thrifty, brave, clean, and reverent" ...

And the Boy Scout Oath is,

"On my honor, I will do my best to do my duty to God and my country, to obey the Scout Laws, to help other people at all times, to keep myself physically strong, mentally awake and morally straight."

Well, if these are not the goals of the people of the United States, what they want their President to live up to, then ... either you have the wrong man or I have the wrong country.

Ford stated at Lenoir Rhyne College, Hickory, North Carolina, March 20, 1976:

I am proud of the fact that I was an Eagle Scout, and I am proud of the Boy Scouts of America.

You know, the Scout Oath, the Scout Laws are the best guidelines I know to give you the right direction in school, in marriage, in your career, to make your life happy and prosperous.

So, if you live up to the Scout Oath and the Scout Laws ... you can't go wrong.

President Ronald Reagan remarked on Private Sector Initiatives at a Briefing for National Service Organization Leaders, April 27, 1982:

After being told for decades that government is the answer, some people's reluctance to try a different approach is understandable.

What if, for example, the Boy Scouts of America were a government program instead of a voluntary activity?

Well, someone's worked out what the answer to that would be. It's been estimated that just doing what the Boy Scouts are doing now ... if run by the government, would cost about $5 1/2 billion a year.

Reagan remarked at a White House Luncheon commemorating the 75th Anniversary of the Boy Scouts of America, February 8, 1985:

Former Scouts have walked on the Moon, become President, and won the Heisman Trophy. Today they serve as Cabinet Secretaries, as my Press Secretary, and in the Congress. In fact, about two-thirds of the Members of the Congress have been in the Boy Scouts ...

How nice it would have been if the Boy Scouts had a merit badge for a balanced budget amendment.

Reagan proclaimed on the 75th Anniversary of the Boy Scouts of America, December 15, 1985:

> The Boy Scouts of America, our Nation's largest organization for young people, has served our youth since 1910. Thanks to dedicated adult volunteers, more than 70 million young people have learned Scouting's lessons of patriotism, courage, and self-reliance over the past 75 years.

President George H.W. Bush remarked at the Boy Scout National Jamboree in Bowling Green, Virginia, August 7, 1989:

> The Boy Scouts have played a leadership role in preparing a generation for space exploration. It's no coincidence that half of all astronauts were once Scouts:
>
> Admiral Richard Truly, who ably heads NASA, is an Eagle Scout; Gus Grissom, an American hero who lost his life in the early space program, was a Scout; David Scott, who operated that first lunar rover, was a Scout; And Jim Lovell, another lunar explorer, whom I'm told is with us today. And I guess, Jim, if you're here, it's true what they say: Once an Eagle Scout, always an Eagle Scout ...
>
> Eagle Scout Neil Armstrong, who made man's first step on the Moon and later sent his greetings to the Jamboree from deep space ...
>
> God bless the Boy Scouts of America.

President Bush stated at James Madison High School, Vienna, Virginia, March 28, 1989:

> People wonder and talk about ... the Thousand Points of Light? ... Helping some kid that may be tempted to use narcotics ... a church group doing something ... It's the Red Cross ... It is the Boy Scouts ... It is Christian Athletes ... Voluntarism.

President Herbert Hoover was supportive of volunteer organizations. During the Great Mississippi Flood of 1927, he successfully organized relief efforts.

Hoover addressed the 20th Anniversary of the Boy Scouts, March 10, 1930:

> The boy ... is a complex of cells teeming with ... curiosity ... The problem ... is what to do with him in his leisure time that will ... contribute to ... his morals ... What will direct his interests to constructive joy instead of destructive glee ... His is the plastic period when indelible impressions must be made.

In his last message to the Boy Scouts, 1929, Sir Robert Baden-Powell wrote:

> Dear Scouts, If you have ever seen the play "Peter Pan," you will remember how the pirate chief was always making his dying speech because he was afraid that possibly when the time came for him to die he might not have time to get it off his chest.
> It is much the same with me, and so, although I am not at this moment dying, I shall be doing so one of these days and I want to send you a parting word of good-bye.

Remember, it is the last you will ever hear from me, so think it over ...

He continued:

I have had a most happy life and I want each one of you to have as happy a life too. I believe that God put us in this jolly world to be happy and enjoy life.

Happiness doesn't come from being rich, nor merely from being successful in your career, nor by self-indulgence.

One step towards happiness is to make yourself healthy and strong while you are a boy, so that you can be useful and so can enjoy life when you are a man.

Nature study will show you how full of beautiful and wonderful things God has made the world for you to enjoy ...

Be contented with what you have got and make the best of it. Look on the bright side of things instead of the gloomy one.

But the real way to get happiness is by giving out happiness to other people. Try and leave this world a little better than you found it, and when your turn comes to die you can die happy in feeling that at any rate you have not wasted your time but have done your best.

"Be Prepared" in this way, to live happy and to die happy — stick to your Scout Promise always — even after you have ceased to be a boy — and God help you to do it.

Your friend, Baden-Powell of Gilwell.

In 2013, a new adventure organization began for young men, Trail Life USA, offering exciting camping, physical and mental challenges, with awards. By 2024, its membership grew to 60,000 members in 1,200 Troops in 50 states.

TrailLifeUSA.com states:

> Trail Life USA is a Church-Based, Christ-Centered, Boy-Focused mentoring and discipleship journey that speaks to the heart of a boy.
>
> Established on timeless values derived from the Bible and set in the context of outdoor adventure, boys from age 5 to 17 are engaged in a Troop setting by male mentors where they are challenged to grow in character, understand their purpose, serve their community, and develop practical leadership skills to carry out the mission for which they were created.

The Trail Life Oath is:

> On my honor, I will do my best,
> To serve God and my country;
> To respect authority;
> To be a good steward of creation;
> And to treat others as I want to be treated.

JULIETTE LOW FOUNDED THE GIRL SCOUTS

Juliette Gordon Low had chronic ear infections as a child, which made one ear deaf. A grain of rice thrown at her wedding in 1886 lodged in her other ear, which was punctured trying to remove it.

Juliette Low's father was a U.S. Army General after being a Confederate captain in the Civil War. Her mother founded the Colonial Dames of Georgia, and brought a Red Cross chapter to Savannah. In the Spanish–American War, Juliette and her mother organized a convalescent hospital for wounded soldiers returning from Cuba.

After an estranged marriage, her husband died in 1905. Juliette Low traveled to England where, in 1911, she met Boer War hero Sir Robert Baden-Powell, founder of the Boy Scouts. His sister, Agnes Baden-Powell, led Girl Guides. Juliette Low joined Girl Guides and became a leader. She formed a troop near her home in Scotland.

On March 12, 1912, Juliette Low brought Girl Guides to America, starting the first two troops in Savannah, Georgia. The next year, she changed the name to Girl Scouts.

The original Girl Scout promise was:

> On my honor, I will try: to do my duty to God and my country, to help other people at all times, to obey the Girl Scout laws.

President Herbert Hoover's wife, First Lady Lou Hoover, was a proponent of women's suffrage and women's rights. She served twice as president of the Girl Scouts of the USA from 1922 to 1925 and again from 1935 to 1937.

As First Lady, she invited the first black woman to dine as an honored guest in the White House – Jessie De Priest, wife of Republican Congressman Oscar Stanton De Priest of Illinois. The Hoovers also had the Tuskegee Institute

Choir perform at the White House.

From the early 20th century on, other organizations were formed, often with church-affiliation: Girls' Guild, Pioneer Girls, Frontier Girls, GEMS Girls Clubs, Pathfinders, Moonbeams, Sunbeams, and Girl Guards.

In 1995, parents in West Chester, Ohio, wanted a new organization for their daughters. This led Patti Garibay to found "American Heritage Girls," a family-friendly organization dedicated to building women of integrity through service to God, family, community and country.

Focusing on "Faith, Service and Fun," the American Heritage Girls' Oath is:

> I promise to love God, Cherish my family, Honor my country, and Serve in my community.

~

TOASTMASTERS

In 1903, Ralph C. Smedley, the education director at the Y.M.C.A. in Bloomington, Illinois, created a speaking program for young adults to help them with communication skills. Since classes resembled the typical toasts that were given at banquets, he gave it the name Toastmasters International.

It did not catch on till he was transferred to the Y.M.C.A. in Santa Ana, California, and organized his first meeting, October 22, 1924. More clubs were formed, and soon there was a federation of Toastmasters. In 1941, Smedley resigned his position at the Y.M.C.A. to devote his full attention to Toastmasters International.

Toastmasters has 16,600 clubs, with 364,000 members in 145 countries. Since its founding, over four million have participated.

DALE CARNEGIE, WIN FRIENDS & INFLUENCE PEOPLE

Dale Carnegie's life was influenced by the Y.M.C.A. in New York City. His life began on a poor farm in Maryville, Missouri, November 24, 1888. He grew up around the town of Bedison and was educated in rural one room school houses in Rose Hill and Harmony.

When he was 16-years-old, his farming family moved to a Warrensburg, Missouri, where his responsibilities included waking up at three in the morning to milk cows and feed pigs. Unfortunately, he lost a finger in a farm machinery accident.

He walked to school, and there, found out he was not able to compete athletically.

Fortunately, though, he discovered he had an aptitude for reciting and debating. He finished high school in 1906, and attended a State Teacher's College.

One day he attended a lecture put on by the touring educational organization, The Chautauqua Institution, based out of Chautauqua Lake, New

York. Notable lecturers included Mark Twain and Susan B. Anthony. This was a growing movement till it was replaced by radio.

Inspired to be a speaker, he attempted to copy the style of the speakers he had heard. Riding his horse to school everyday, he would practice his speaking style. He entered intercollegiate speaking competitions, winning many of them. Some students even paid him to coach them in how to speak.

His first job after graduating was in Alliance, Nebraska, 1908, going to farmers and ranchers and selling them courses with the International Correspondence Schools. He then worked for the meat packing Armour and Company, and became quite successful selling lard and soap in South Omaha, Nebraska.

By 1911, he had saved up five hundred dollars to pursue his goal. He quit his job, traveled to New York, and attended the American Academy of Dramatic Arts. He was in the road show Polly of the Circus, playing the part of Dr. Hartley. Once the production came to an end, he realized that theater life was not what he wanted.

He rented a room at the Y.M.C.A., on 125th Street in New York. This is where he got the idea in 1912 to teach a biblically-based class at the Y.M.C.A. on how to be a public speaker.

He negotiated with the manager so that he would charge the attendees a fee, and give twenty percent that to the Y.M.C.A. He quickly taught students how to interview well, make persuasive presentations, and nurture positive relationships.

Soon, though he taught everything he knew, but to keep the class going and to get shy students to participate, he improvised, suggesting students take turns speaking out about "something that made them angry."

To his amazement, this was a key. Students soon were unafraid to address a public group.

He developed the Dale Carnegie Course, which helped ordinary people have self-confidence. In 1913, he published *Public Speaking and Influencing Men of Business.*

Carnegie had tapped into the average American's desire to have more self-confidence. By 1914, his weekly take home pay was $500, equivalent to around $15,000 today.

In 1915, he published with Joseph Berg Esenwein, *The Art of Public Speaking,* writing:

> "Destiny is not a matter of chance. It is a matter of choice."

> "The first sign of greatness is when a man does not attempt to look and act great. Before you can call yourself a man at all, Kipling assures us, you must 'not look too good nor talk too wise.'"

He served for a year and a half in the U.S. Army during World War I, but due to his finger accident as a youth he was assigned to an office job at Camp Upton in Long Island, New York.

He worked as the business manager for the speaking tour of Lowell Thomas, a broadcaster made famous for covering Lawrence of Arabia.

In 1916, he organized a lecture at Carnegie Hall. To his amazement, it sold out. The success of this event influenced him to change the spelling of his last name from Carnagey to Carnagie, to match the more recognizable name of the benefactor of Carnagie Hall, steel industrialist Andrew Carnegie.

In 1920, he published Public Speaking: the Standard Course of the United Y.M.C.A. Schools.

In 1926, he published *Public Speaking: a Practical Course for Business Men*, renamed *Public Speaking and Influencing Men in Business* in 1932. In 1927, he married Lolita Baucaire, but sadly it did not last and they divorced in 1931.

In 1932, he published *Lincoln the Unknown*, and in 1934, *Little Known Facts About Well Known People*. His most well-known book, *How to Win Friends and Influence People*, was published in 1935 by Simon & Schuster. Selling for just two dollars, it was an instant best-seller, being translated into 31 languages and selling over 30 million copies. In it, he wrote:

> "Winning friends begins with friendliness."

> "A dog makes his living by giving you nothing but love. You can make more friends in two months by becoming interested in other people than you can in two years by trying to get other people interested in you."

> "To be interesting, be interested."

> "'If there is any one secret of success,' said Henry Ford, 'it lies in the ability to get the other person's point of view and see things from that person's angle as well as from your own.'"

"If we want to make friends, let's put ourselves out to do things for other people—things that require time, energy, unselfishness and thoughtfulness."

"The world is full of people who are ... self-seeking. So the rare individual who unselfishly tries to serve others has an enormous advantage."

"It is the individual who is not interested in his fellow men who has the greatest difficulties in life and provides the greatest injury to others. It is from among such individuals that all human failures spring."

"The deepest principle in human nature is the craving to be appreciated."

"Remember that a person's name is to that person the sweetest and most important sound in any language."

"'People who smile,' he said, 'tend to manage, teach and sell more effectively, and to raise happier children.'"

"Actions speak louder than words, and a smile says, 'I like you. You make me happy. I am glad to see you.' That is why dogs make such a hit. They are so glad to see us that they almost jump out of their skins. So, naturally, we are glad to see them."

"Talk to someone about themselves and they'll listen for hours."

"Emerson said: 'Every man I meet is my superior in some way. In that, I learn of him.'"

"The secret of his success? 'I will speak ill of no man,' he said, '... and speak all the good I know of everybody.'"

"John Wanamaker, founder of the department stores that bear his name, once confessed: 'I learned thirty years ago that it is foolish to scold. I have enough trouble overcoming my own limitations without fretting over the fact that God has not seen fit to distribute evenly the gift of intelligence.'"

"To change somebody's behavior, change the level of respect she receives by giving her a fine reputation to live up to. Act as though the trait you are trying to influence is already one of the person's outstanding characteristics."

"Control your temper. Remember, you can measure the size of a person by what makes him or her angry."

"If you argue and rankle and contradict, you may achieve a victory sometimes; but it will be an empty victory because you will never get your opponent's good will."

"Instead of condemning people, let's try to understand them. Let's try to figure out why they do what they do. That's a lot more profitable and intriguing than criticism; and it breeds sympathy, tolerance and kindness. 'To know all is to forgive all.'"

"You can't win an argument. You can't because if you lose it, you lose it; and if you win it, you lose it."

"A man convinced against his will – Is of the same opinion still."

"There is only one way under high heaven to get the best of an argument – and that is to avoid it."

"I have come to the conclusion that there is only one way under high heaven to get the best of an argument— and that is to avoid it. Avoid it as you would avoid rattlesnakes and earthquakes."

"If you want to gather honey, don't kick over the beehive."

"If your temper is aroused and you tell 'em a thing or two, you will have a fine time unloading your feelings. But what about the other fellow? Will he share your pleasure? Will your belligerent tones, your hostile attitude, make it easy for him to agree with you? ... 'If you come at me with your fists doubled,' said Woodrow Wilson, 'I think I can promise you that mine will double as fast as yours ...

but if you come to me and say, "Let us sit down and take counsel together, and, if we differ from one another, understand why it is that we differ from one another, just what the points at issue are," we will presently find that we are not so far apart after all, that the points on which we differ are few and the points on which we agree are many, and that if we only have the patience and the candor and the desire to get together, we will get together.'"

"If you disagree with them, you may be tempted to interrupt. But don't. It's dangerous. They won't pay attention to you while they still have a lot of ideas of theirs crying for expression. So listen patiently and with an open mind. Be sincere about it. Encourage them to express their ideas fully. They will never forget. And you will learn a thing or two."

"Nobody is more persuasive than a good listener."

"Any fool can criticize, complain, and condemn—and most fools do. But it takes character and self-control to be understanding and forgiving."

"People who can put themselves in the place of other people, who can understand the workings of their minds, need never worry about what the future has in store for them."

"You cannot teach a man anything; you can only help him to find it within himself."

"Letting the other person feel that the idea is his or hers not only works in business and politics, it works in family life as well."

"'All men have fears, but the brave put down their fears and go forward, sometimes to death, but always to victory' was the motto of the King's Guard in ancient Greece."

"First ask yourself: What is the worst that can happen? Then prepare to accept it. Then proceed to improve on the worst."

"If you want to conquer fear, don't sit at home and think about it. Go out and get busy."

In 1936, he published *The Little Golden Book*, which was later renamed *The Golden Book*.

After reading hundreds of biographies of the world's greatest leaders, he published *Five Minute Biographies*, 1937; *How to Get Ahead in the World Today*, 1938; and *Dale Carnegie's Biographical Roundup*, 1944.

On November 5, 1944, he married his former secretary, Dorothy Price Vanderpool, in Tulsa, Oklahoma, adopting her daughter, Rosemary. They had a daughter together, Donna Dale. Dorothy was instrumental in expanding the organization. He published *How to Put Magic in the Magic Formula*, 1946; and *A Quick and Easy Way to Learn to Speak in Public*, 1947.

Dale Carnegie wrote in *How to Stop Worrying and Start Living: Time–Tested Methods for Conquering Worry*, 1948:

"The best possible way to prepare for tomorrow is to concentrate with all your intelligence, all your enthusiasm, on doing today's work superbly today! That is the only possible way you can prepare for the future."

"Let's not allow ourselves to be upset by small things we should despise and forget. Remember 'Life is too short to be little.'"

"Let's never try to get even with our enemies, because if we do we will hurt ourselves far more than we hurt them. Let's do as General Eisenhower does: let's never waste a minute thinking about people we don't like."

"When I asked him – Mr. Henry Ford – if he ever worried, he replied: 'No. I believe God is managing affairs and that He doesn't need any advice from me. With God in charge, I believe that everything will work out for the best in the end. So what is there to worry about?'"

"If you want to keep happiness , you have to share it !"

"If You Have A Lemon, Make Lemonade. That is what a great educator does. But the fool does the exact opposite. If he finds that life has handed him a lemon, he gives up and says: 'I'm beaten. It is fate. I haven't got a chance.' Then he proceeds to rail against the world and indulge in an orgy of self-pity.
But when the wise man is handed a lemon, he says: 'What lesson can I learn from this misfortune? How can I improve my situation? How can I turn this lemon into a lemonade?'"

> "When we hate our enemies, we are giving them power over us: power over our sleep, our appetites, our blood pressure, our health, and our happiness."

In *How to Stop Worrying and Start Living: Time–Tested Methods for Conquering Worry*, 1948, Carnegie gave an encouragement in faith:

> "The words 'Think and Thank' are inscribed in many of the Cromwellian churches of England. These words ought to be inscribed in our hearts, too: 'Think and Thank.' Think of all we have to be grateful for, and thank God for all our boons and bounties."

> "Relaxation and recreation: The most relaxing recreating forces are a healthy religion, sleep, music, and laughter. Have faith in God—learn to sleep well— Love good music—see the funny side of life— And health and happiness will be yours."

Carnegie shared an eternal perspective in *How to Stop Worrying and Start Living*, 1948:

> When we are harassed and reach the limit of our own strength, many of us then turn in desperation to God – "There are no atheists in foxholes."
>
> But why wait till we are desperate? Why not renew our strength every day? Why wait even until Sunday?
>
> For years I have had the habit of dropping into empty churches on weekday afternoons ... When I feel that I am too rushed and hurried to spare a few minutes to think about spiritual things, I say to

myself:

"Wait a minute, Dale Carnegie, wait a minute. Why all the feverish hurry and rush, little man? You need to pause and acquire a little perspective."

At such times, I frequently drop into the first church that I find open ...

Although I am a Protestant, I frequently, on weekday afternoons, drop into St. Patrick's Cathedral on Fifth Avenue, and remind myself that I'll be dead in another thirty years, but that the great spiritual truths that all churches teach are eternal. I close my eyes and pray.

I find that doing this calms my nerves, rests my body, clarifies my perspective, and helps me revalue my values. May I recommend this practice to you?

He wrote his last book in 1952, *How to Make Our Listeners Like Us*. By the time of his death at the age of 66, on November 1, 1955, over 450,000 had taken his courses which were conducted in 750 cities and in 15 countries. After his death, his wife, Dorothy, continued publishing his material.

Motivational speakers that continued in sharing positive messages include Pastor Norman Vincent Peale of New York's historic Marble Collegiate Dutch Reformed Church, and Dutch Reformed Pastor Robert Schuller, who built the Crystal Cathedral in Garden Grove, California.

Carnegie's advice can be summed up as:

> "Develop success from failures. Discouragement and failure are two of the surest stepping stones to success."

"Forget yourself; do things for others."

Dale Carnegie wrote in *How to Win Friends & Influence People:*

> Most of the important things in the world have been accomplished by people who have kept on trying when there seemed to be no hope at all.

∽

Y.M.C.A. DURING DEPRESSION AND WORLD WAR II

The Y.M.C.A. was initially run by volunteers and focused on evangelism, street preaching, safe boarding houses and discipling young men.

During the Civil War, Spanish-American War, and World War I, the Y.M.C.A. began to be involved in relief and service programs.

When the Great Depression began, the Y.M.C.A. engaged in aid and benevolence efforts, extending a helping-hand to the down and out.

President Herbert Hoover led a drive to mobilize Christian organizations to provide relief, October 18, 1931:

> This great complex, which we call American life, is builded and can alone survive upon the translation into individual action of that fundamental philosophy announced by the Savior nineteen centuries ago ... Modern society cannot survive with the defense of Cain, 'Am I my brother's keeper?'"

Then President Franklin D. Roosevelt instituted the New Deal with federal government welfare. This resulted in the Y.M.C.A. and other non-profit aid organizations reevaluating their mission.

Some chapters began to focus on community projects, others emphasized exercise, recreation and camping, others offered free medical assistance, and still others provided educational classes on an array of subjects and vocational training classes to prepare men to return to work.

In 1932, a Leisure Time League program at the Y.M.C.A. in Minneapolis drew thousands to "unite unemployed young men who desire to maintain their physical and mental vigor and wish to train themselves for greater usefulness and service to themselves and the community."

In 1939, as World War II began, women were engaged in the Y.M.C.A.–USO programs. In 1940, women served on the Y.M.C.A. National Council's Army and Navy Department committee.

In 1941, a special council committee was formed – "Principles and Standards of Y.M.C.A. Work with Women and Girls"

In 1942, the GSO, Girls Service Organization, reached an enrollment of 100,000. By 1946, approximately 62 percent of Y.M.C.A.s allowed female members, and women made up 12 percent of Y.M.C.A.'s membership.

During World War II, the Y.M.C.A. printed and distributed millions of Bibles and prayer books to U.S. soldiers and sailors:

> The New Testament – An American Translation–Special Edition published for the Army and Navy Department by

The National Board of the Young Men's Christian Associations — One of the Agencies of the United States Service Organization — *Association Press*, 247 Madison Avenue, New York (June 1942).

The Gideons International printed a New Testament and Book of Psalms given out to the millions of U.S. soldiers and sailors. President Roosevelt wrote the foreword, January 25, 1941:

> As Commander-in-Chief, I take pleasure in commending the reading of the Bible to all who serve in the armed forces of the United States ...
>
> Throughout the centuries, men of many faiths and diverse origins have found in the Sacred Book words of wisdom, counsel and inspiration.
>
> It is a fountain of strength and now, as always, an aid in attaining the highest aspirations of the human soul.
> –(signed) Franklin D. Roosevelt.

From 1939 to 1945, the Y.M.C.A. undertook humanitarian tasks similar to what it had done in World War I. The work of the War Prisoners Aid Program was of greater magnitude and duration than anything before it, caring for 6 million POWs, prisoners of war, in camps in 36 countries

Beginning in 1942, it helped care for 110,000 Japanese Americans in ten interment camps. David M. Tatsuno, an internee who had been a member of the San Francisco Y.M.C.A., said during this difficult time, "The Y never forgot us." Tatsuno's film footage of the interment camp in Topaz, Utah, is in the Library of Congress.

Roosevelt asked the Y.M.C.A. to mobilize support for the military by coordinating the Red Cross, The Salvation Army, National Catholic Community Services, Jewish Welfare Board, and National Travelers Aid Association into the United Services Organizations, or USO.

In 1947, the USO was deactivated, and the Y.M.C.A.'s Army and Navy Department immediately filled the gap in social services for military personnel. The next year, the Y.M.C.A. Armed Services Department assumed responsibility for 26 former USO branches and established work overseas.

In 1951, the USO was reactivated during the Korean War, with the Y.M.C.A. serving as its major operating agency, continuing operations through the Vietnam conflict, and in different capacities up through the present.

Y.M.C.A.'s humanitarian programs were copied by The Peace Corp, formed in 1960 by President John F. Kennedy.

FELLOWSHIP OF CHRISTIAN ATHLETES

Millions of young men and women athletes are inspired by the Fellowship of Christian Athletes, founded by Don McClanen.

Born February 23, 1925. Don served in the U.S. Navy in the Pacific during World War II. After the war, Don and his wife Gloria went to

Oklahoma State University where he studied to be a coach. His youth pastor asked him to consider incorporating his faith with his sports career.

Questioning how, he heard a speaker at an education conference in Oklahoma City challenging them, that they can either lead youth "up a mountain or down a drain." While on a walk, he felt drawn to enter a small church where he prayed "Lord, I surrender my will to You."

After graduation, he coached at a high school in Stillwater, OK, then at Eastern Oklahoma State. Reading that there were 30 million unchurched, youth, he began posting newspaper clippings of Christian athletes and coaches in the locker room, and held prayer meetings before games.

In 1954, McClanen met former Occidental College basketball player, Pastor Louis H. Evans, named by *LIFE magazine* as one of America's top 10 clergymen. McClanen shared his goals:

> If athletes can endorse shaving cream, razor blades and cigarettes, surely they can endorse the Lord.

Evans advised McClanen to write to the athletes he had read about to see if they would back:

> ... some type of organization that would provide an opportunity for those of us who are so inclined to speak and witness for Christ and the wholesome principles of good character and clean living to the youth of our nation.

In August of 1954, McClanen met Branch Rickey, general manager of the Pittsburgh Pirates, renown for knocking down the color barrier by signing Jackie Robinson to the Brooklyn Dodgers. McClanen said of the meeting:

> Finally, he made a statement that I'll never forget ... "This thing has the potential of changing the youth scene of America within a decade. It is pregnant with potential. It is just ingenious. It's a new thing; where has it been?"

Rickey connected McClanen with Pittsburgh Businessman Paul Benedum who donated seed money. In September of 1954, they held the first advisory board meeting in Oklahoma City, resolving that "Christian" should be the emphasis, not just "religious." Three months later, November 10, 1954, the Fellowship of Christian Athletes was chartered.

McClanen organized school assemblies and invited famous Christian athletes and coaches to speak, including Amos Alonzo Stagg, the Grand Old Man of Football. In the next few years, city-wide events were held in Oklahoma City, Tulsa, Denver, Houston, and Indianapolis, with over 90,000 young people hearing the Gospel.

The first FCA National Conference was held at the Y.M.C.A. of the Rockies in Estes Park, Colorado, August of 1956, with 256 attendees. The theme was Jesus' words, "I am the Way, the Truth, and the Life." The event was reported by *Life Magazine*, *Newsweek*, *Sports Illustrated* and *Guideposts*, with messages sent from President Dwight D. Eisenhower and Secretary of State John Foster Dulles.

Starting with just a dream, Don and Gloria McClanen prayed they would not go bankrupt as he was still working as athletic director at Eastern Oklahoma State while they grew FCA. Their son, Douglas, died a day old, and daughter, Judy, died at age 10. Don and Gloria had two other children, Michael and Laurie, and many grandchildren.

In 1961, McClanen passed the baton of leadership, and since then the FCA has grown to reach millions of young men and women athletes for Christ in over 90 countries.

FCA President Les Steckel wrote of founder Don McClanen:

> If there is ever a question about what God can do with a life totally surrendered, called and risking all to follow His vision, we can point to a young basketball coach from Oklahoma, who in 1954 saw the potential of athletes and coaches to share the Gospel with the world.
>
> Years later, that vision is alive and well through FCA, influencing lives for Christ across the globe—an amazing legacy.
>
> We praise God for the life of Don McClanen. His unwavering commitment and vision truly enabled FCA to grow to where it is today, encouraging millions of coaches and athletes to lead lives dedicated to Christ.

An example of FCA's impact at Purdue University was Joe Bell ('70), a track star running hurdles in the Big Ten Conference. Seeking direction, his coach explained the Gospel which profoundly influenced his life. Joe eventually became pastor of Calvary Chapel Lafayette, Indiana, a church with an international outreach.

Another organization, Athletes in Action, was founded in 1966 with the help of Dave Hannah.

It is the international sports ministry of Cru, a Christian evangelism and discipleship organization. AIA not only challenges athletes to the highest levels of competitive excellence, but empowers them to be leaders and Christ-centered influencers on and off the field.

Athletes in Action is on more than 205 college campuses in 97 countries. Its professional sports teams compete around the globe with players and coaches often sharing testimonies at half-time.

AIA's NFL Ministry serves players, coaches, alumni, executives and their families, helping them grow in relationship with God and community. Through sports media, AIA touches an estimated 100 million people annually.

One AIA athlete was Jerry Perera, who at Eastern Nazarene College ('79) amassed 1,332 points in 110 basketball games, recognized as an NCCAA All-American and Associated Press' All-American Honorable Mention. He played on the NBA SoCal Summer Pro League and then traveled the globe witnessing his faith as a player on the Athletes in Action USA/Canada team.

STRENGTH TO DO YOUR DUTY

Webster's 1828 Dictionary defined:

> DUTY: That which a person owes to another; that which a person is

> bound, by any natural, moral or legal obligation, to pay, do or perform.

A renown story of a young person doing his duty was during the Revolution when General George Washington was desperate to know British plans. 21-year-old Yale graduate, Nathan Hale, volunteered to go into British-occupied New York as a spy.

Sadly, a British loyalist recognized him and he was arrested. Nathan Hale was hung, September 22, 1776, but not without uttering his last words which inspired the new nation with courage:

> I only regret that I have but one life to lose for my country.

General Washington composed a "Circular to the States," January 31, 1782:

> The race is not always to the swift, nor the battle to the strong; yet, without presumptuously waiting for miracles to be wrought in our favor, it is our indispensable duty, with the deepest gratitude to Heaven for the past, and humble confidence in its smiles on our future operations, to make use of all the means in our power for our defense.

One of history's greatest naval battles was the Battle of Trafalgar, October 21, 1805. When Napoleon's combined French and Spanish fleet sought to invade England, British Admiral Horatio Nelson stopped him.

Over ten thousand were killed or wounded in the fighting, with ships ripped apart at point-blank range by cannonade and musket shot.

As victory neared, British Admiral Nelson was

fatally shot in the spine and carried below deck to the ship's surgeon, uttering his dying words:

> Thank God I have done my duty.

World War I flying ace Eddie Rickenbacker said:

> I want to make it clear that this escape and the others were not the result of any super ability or knowledge on my part. I wouldn't be alive today if I had to depend on that. I realized then, as I headed for France on one wing, that there had to be something else ...
>
> I had seen others die, brighter and more able than I. I knew there was a power. I believe in calling upon it for aid and for guidance.
>
> I am not such an egotist as to believe that God has spared me because I am I. I believe there is work for me to do and that I am spared to do it, just as you are.

On October 29, 1941, after months of Nazi bombardments which destroyed 2 million houses in London, Winston Churchill addressed the students of London's Harrow School, a boys' boarding school run with the discipline of Thomas Arnold's Rugby School:

> You cannot tell from appearances how things will go .... People who are imaginative see many more dangers than perhaps exist ... but then they must also pray to be given that extra courage ...
>
> I am addressing myself to the School — surely from this period of ten months this is the lesson: never give in, never give in, never, never, never, never — in

nothing, great or small, large or petty — never give in except to convictions of honor and good sense.

Never yield to force; never yield to the apparently overwhelming might of the enemy. We stood all alone a year ago, and to many countries it seemed that ... we were finished ...

But instead our country stood in the gap. There was no flinching and no thought of giving in; and by what seemed almost a miracle ... we now find ourselves in a position where I say that we can be sure that we have only to persevere to conquer.

This attitude was echoed by President Donald J. Trump, who, after having survived two assassination attempts, stated in his Second Inaugural Address, January 20, 2025:

> God spared my life for a reason — to save our country and restore America to greatness.

British Journalist Piers Morgan interviewed Dana White, president of the Ultimate Fighting Championship, February 3, 2025:

> Dana: "We talk about what it means to be a fighter. Now nobody embodies that more than President Trump. I mean ... This guy was this close to being assassinated and the way he fought through that and bounced back from it."
>
> Piers: "... The iconic image of that whole campaign was when he got shot standing up and saying fight, fight, fight!

When you saw that what did you think?"

Dana: "I was flying to Italy when that happened and my wife woke me up and said they just shot President Trump ... When I landed I called him and he was already home from the hospital and unfazed."

Piers: "When you spoke to him that night what did you say to him?"

Dana: "Why are you doing this ... Give it up. I told him stop so many times ... You have such a good life and you could do all these other things. But the thing is with President Trump is, he believes, he believes in God and he's very, you know, he's very religious."

Piers: "He told me he thinks God must have had a plan for me. He wanted me to survive that bullet."

Dana: "He believes that to his core, that God has spared his life to be the President, and do the things that he's going to do over the next four years "

Piers: "When you said to just give it up, what did he say to you?"
Dana: "I can't quit. You don't ever quit. You never quit!"

SENATE CHAPLAIN PETER MARSHALL, NEED FOR HEROES

U.S. Senate Peter Marshall gave a challenge (*20 Centuries of Great Preaching,* Word, 1971):

> The history of the world has always been the biography of her great men ...
>
> There was a time in these United States when youth was inspired by heroes ... when a picture of Washington or Lincoln adorned every school room wall ...
>
> Along with the ponderous Family Bible on the Victorian table and the hymn books on the old-fashioned square piano, there looked down from the walls the likenesses of our national heroes ...
>
> Those were the days of great beliefs – belief in the authority of the Scriptures, belief that prayer was really answered, belief in marriage and the family as permanent institutions, belief in the integrity and worth of America's great men.
>
> These beliefs laid the groundwork for producing more great men, for many a boy figured, "If that man could do it, get an education, make his life count for something, then I can too ..."

Marshall continued:

> Then there dawned the day when the pictures of Washington and Lincoln did not fit in with our concept of modern décor ... The old Family Bible looked embarrassingly out of place ... So the pictures and the Bible were often relegated to the Attic of Forgotten Things.

> There went with them some of the most stabilizing influences of American life.
>
> We had become a more sophisticated people, somewhat cynical of the cherished beliefs of our ancestors, rather blasé, frankly skeptical of old-fashioned sentimentalism.
>
> Along with our higher education came a debunking contest. This debunking became a sort of national sport ... It was smarter to revile than to revere ... more fashionable to depreciate than to appreciate.
>
> In our classrooms at all levels of education, no longer did we laud great men — those who had struggled and achieved. Instead, we merely took their dimensions and ferreted out their faults.
>
> We decided that it was silly to say God sent them for a special task ... They were merely ... products of their environments ... The Constitution, that hitherto cherished charter of American liberties, was drawn up by men who never spoke on a telephone or flew in a plane, therefore, we should change the Constitution to suit modern ways.

Thomas Sowell, a Senior Fellow at the Hoover Institution at Stanford University, stated:

> Ours may become the first civilization destroyed, not by the power of our enemies, but by the ignorance of our teachers and the dangerous nonsense they are teaching our children. In an age of artificial intelligence, they are creating artificial stupidity.

Actor John Wayne put it more bluntly:

> "Life is tough, but it's tougher if you're stupid."

"All battles are fought by scared men who'd rather be some place else."

"Courage is being scared to death, but saddling up anyway."

Senate Chaplain Marshall continued:

We failed to realize that when we were denying the existence of great men, we were also denying the desirability of great men.

So now, many of our children have grown up without the guiding star ... holding in their hands only a bunch of ... question marks, with no keys with which to open the doors of knowledge and life.

The young no longer have any particular ambition to become heroes. Their ambition now was to make as much money as possible, as quickly as possible, in whatever way was most convenient ...

Thus, our debunking is ... a sign of decaying foundations of character to the individual and in the national life ...

We who are Christians, believe that God gives the world a few great men to lead the rest of us closer to Him, that to depreciate or to deny their greatness is to deny one of God's revelations of Himself to mankind.

The heroes the Christian cherishes ... were (or are) human .. They have their weakness ... Their faults are well-known to their friends, better known to themselves.

But the point is that with God and His guidance, they can provide the moral leadership that our nation so sorely needs.

America needs heroes on the battlefield of everyday life ... in our homes, in our schools, on college campuses, in offices and factories, who can lead us towards a return to idealism. For time is running out for us ...

Peter Marshall concluded:

The call today is for Christian heroes and heroines ... who are willing to speak a good word for Jesus Christ ... who are willing to live by the undiluted values of Christian morality in the pagan atmosphere of our society surrounded by lewdness, pornography, and profanity.

This may be a higher bravery than that of any battlefield: to face ridicule, sarcasm, sneering disdain for what one believes to be right.

To fight for goodness and right ... fighting the battle first in our own hearts and souls ... seeking God's help to overcome our particular temptations for the sake of peace .. for the sake of America ... for our own sake ... for God's sake."

ERIKA KIRK – A COMMISSIONING

Erika Kirk, on behalf of her husband, Charlie Kirk, received from President Donald J. Trump the Presidential Medal of Freedom, October 14, 2025, stating:

Charlie often said that without God, freedom becomes chaos ... that the freest people in the world are those whose hearts belong to Christ ... Freedom divorced from faith eventually just destroys itself ... He wanted them to see that liberty isn't self-indulgence, it's self-governance, under God ...

He was never afraid ... always without fear ... He stood for truth, and stood for freedom ... He stood for God when it was costly ... Surprisingly ... he did pray for his enemies. Which is very hard ...

This is not a ceremony. This is a commissioning ... I want you to free yourself from fear. I want you to stand courageously in the truth. Listen for the still, small voice of God ...

God began a mighty work through my husband and I intend to see it through ... Charlie's life was proof that freedom is not a theory, it's a testimony. He showed us that liberty begins not in the halls of power, but in the heart of a man surrendered to God.

GENERAL MACARTHUR – A FATHER'S PRAYER

After World War II, General Douglas MacArthur helped distribute 43 million Bibles in Japan. He worked with Prince Takamatsu, younger brother of Emperor Shōwa, to found the International Christian University, June 15, 1949, located at the Y.M.C.A. Camp in Gotemba, Japan.

It was Japan's first liberal arts college, established for the purpose of raising up Christian leaders.

As the school's Honorary Chairman, MacArthur advocated for the spread of Christianity:

> ... (to) provide the surest foundation for the firm establishment of democracy.

MacArthur told James F. Boughton, November 22, 1947:

> Democracy and Christianity have much in common, as practice of the former is impossible without giving faithful service to the fundamental concepts underlying the latter.

Michael Schaller wrote in *Douglas MacArthur: The Far Eastern General* (1989):

> Christianity often seemed a metaphor for MacArthur's vision of postwar Asia. His most important mission, he told (Defense Secretary) James Forrestal was to secure Asia for Christianity and deny it to Marxism.

Douglas MacArthur warned in a speech to the Salvation Army, December 12, 1951:

> History fails to record a single precedent in which nations subject to moral decay have not passed into political and economic decline. There has been either a spiritual awakening to overcome the moral lapse, or a progressive deterioration leading to ultimate national disaster.

On Father's Day, 1988, Ronald Reagan said:

> Children, vulnerable and dependent, desperately need security, and it has ever been a duty and a joy of fatherhood to offer

it. Being a father requires strength ... and more than a little courage ... to persevere, to fight discouragement, and to keep working for the family ...

With God's grace, fathers find the patience to teach, the fortitude to provide, the compassion to comfort, and the mercy to forgive. All of this is to say that they find the strength to love their wives and children selflessly.

American Indians had a name for a man who proved he had courage to defend his family without regard for his own life – a "brave."

Dr. Ben Carson explained:

> The more solid the family ... the more likely you are to be able to resist peer pressure ... Human beings are social creatures. We all want to belong, we all have that desire, and we will belong, one way or another ... If the family doesn't provide that, the peers will, or a gang will, or you will find something to belong to.

In 1942, General MacArthur was named Father of the Year. He stated:

> By profession I am a soldier and take pride in that fact. But I am prouder — infinitely prouder — to be a father.
>
> A soldier destroys in order to build; the father only builds, never destroys. The one has the potentiality of death; the other embodies creation and life. And while the hordes of death are mighty, the battalions of life are mightier still.
>
> It is my hope that my son, when I am gone, will remember me not from the battle

but in the home repeating with him our simple daily prayer, 'Our Father Who Art in Heaven.'

General MacArthur wrote "A Father's Prayer":

Build me a son, O Lord, who will be strong enough to know when he is weak, brave enough to face himself when he is afraid, one who will be proud and unbending in honest defeat, and humble and gentle in victory.

Build me a son whose wishes will not take the place of deeds; a son who will know Thee — and that to know himself is the foundation stone of knowledge.

Lead him, I pray, not in the path of ease and comfort, but under the stress and spur of difficulties and challenge.

Here let him learn to stand up in the storm; here let him learn compassion for those who fail ...

Build me a son whose heart will be clear, whose goal will be high; a son who will master himself before he seeks to master other men; one who will reach into the future, yet never forget the past.

And after all these things are his, add, I pray, enough of a sense of humor, so that he may always be serious, yet never take himself too seriously.

Give him humility, so that he may always remember the simplicity of true greatness, the open mind of true wisdom, and the meekness of true strength.

Then, I, his father, will dare to whisper, "I have not lived in vain."

www.ingramcontent.com/pod-product-compliance
Lightning Source LLC
Chambersburg PA
CBHW050129170426
43197CB00011B/1762